Servings with Love

Desserts Galore and much, much more

by Elizabeth Pistole

with daughters

Cynthia Poikonen and Carole Bagwell

ISBN 0-87162-223-8

Table of Contents

THE JOY OF—

Human beings are unique in their ability to use imagination and memory. To recall or recognize gives meaning and stability to one's own unique life. It is good practice in the stress of everyday living to take time to remember. One way is to sit quietly; close your eyes and go back to your childhood. See yourself in your home and "experience" the sights, sounds, and smells. Cindy and Carole did this and remembered:

Cynthia

—warm gingerbread or hot chicken noodle soup mother would have for me when I came home from school. Tasted especially good in the winter when I had to ride my bike to my piano lesson.

—daddy always taking the "birthday" child out for breakfast.

—Monday was daddy's day off when he was a pastor and he and mother went to the grocery store. I loved seeing all the good food when I came home, but I did not like the mess all over the table.

—visiting both my grandmothers and eating the roast beef and brown gravy that Mama Smith made. When we packed to leave she always made us fresh hot biscuits and loaded them with butter and jelly. The only problem was that we always had them eaten before we were out of the city limits. Mom Pistole would bring home delicious bakery goods from where she worked. Chocolate buttercream cake was (and is) my favorite.

—the woman who gave us a homemade loaf of bread every Sunday morning after church. We waited in the car for my dad, and we usually ate most of it before we got home. Delicious!

Carole

—daddy giving me two quarters every Saturday morning to ride my bike to the local bakery for one dozen yeast doughnuts. In our family that meant two each; any who ate more got clobbered.

—table games and hot buttered popcorn with the whole family on Friday nights. I wonder how many bushels we consumed.

—mother making a double batch of chicken and dumplings so I could eat all I wanted. (They were rolled out and cut in strips.)

—Making pizza with friends—blindfolded—for my high school psychology class project.

—the rest of the family suffering (not always silently) as I tried my culinary skills and served them baked bananas and other "goodies."

The boys asked to be included and they remembered: entertaining children from the orphanage on special days; having Christmas celebrations three times—at home at Papa and Mama Smith's, and at Mom Pistole's; "pigs in the blanket" for birthday parties (⅓ hot dog wrapped with ½ tube biscuit); and homemade cinnamon rolls.

To keep macaroni from boiling over, put a tablespoon or so of shortening in the water.

Before grating cheese, put a small amount of cooking oil on the grater with either a small pastry brush or a paper towel and rub a bit. When washing the grater . . . all cheese will immediately come off.

If you have trouble getting corn to pop, place the bag or can of popcorn in the deep freeze or freezing compartment of the refrigerator for at least twenty-four hours before using it. The corn will pop up large and tender.

To get the last bit of shortening out of the can, fill it with boiling water, then let it cool. The shortening will rise to the top and harden for easy removal.

When cooking rice, add a spoonful of vinegar or the same amount of lemon juice, and it will be light, separated, and fluffy.

After peeling a cucumber, take a fork and scrape the side from top to bottom. Scrape down hard. Then slice your cucumber. This will leave a little design around each slice. So pretty and easy.

If the filling for your berry pie seems a little too sweet or flat, add the juice of one-half lemon. This not only takes away the too-sweet taste but brings out the flavor of the berries.

When icing a cake (either cooked or powdered sugar icing), if you will dip the knife in hot water before spreading the icing, it will go on smoothly and will not stick to the knife.

CAKES

ICING

Cakes

Poppy Seed Cake

1 package white or yellow cake mix
1 cup water
½ cup liquid shortening
4 eggs
1 package instant coconut cream or lemon pudding mix (3¾-ounce size)
4 T. poppy seeds.

Mix the dry ingredients. Add water and liquid shortening. Add the eggs one at a time, beating well after each one. Pour into a well-greased and floured Bundt pan. Bake at 350° for 45 minutes. Allow the cake to cool in the pan for 15 minutes. This cake does not need frosting, but you may "drizzle" it with a confectionary sugar glaze if you wish.

Westhaven Cake

Makes 12 servings

1 8-ounce package pitted dates
1 t. baking soda
1 cup hot water
½ cup margarine, softened
1 cup sugar
2 eggs
1 t. vanilla extract
1⅓ cups unsifted all-purpose flour
2 T. cocoa

1 6-ounce package semisweet chocolate pieces
½ cup chopped walnuts

Preheat oven to 350°. Grease and flour 9-inch tube pan or 9x13 cake pan.

Cut up dates and place in small bowl. Sprinkle on soda and pour on hot water; set aside. In large mixer bowl, with mixer at medium speed, cream margarine and sugar, scraping bowl occasionally. Beat in eggs and vanilla. Combine flour and cocoa and add to butter mixture. Stir date mixture and pour into flour mixture; continue beating just until mixed. Fold in half of the chocolate pieces and nuts; reserve the rest for the top. Pour into prepared pan; sprinkle on remaining nuts and chocolate. Bake 55 minutes for tube pan; 45 minutes for 13x9-inch pan. Cool completely in pan on wire rack.

"One today is worth two tomorrows; What I am to be I am now becoming."
—Benjamin Franklin

Two-Egg Treasure Cake

2 cups sifted cake flour
1⅓ cups sugar
2½ t. baking powder
1 t. salt
½ cup shortening
1 cup less 2 T. milk
1½ t. vanilla
2 eggs, unbeaten

Sift dry ingredients into mixing bowl. Drop in shortening. Add ⅔ of milk, then vanilla, and beat for 2 minutes on low speed of mixer. Add eggs and remaining milk and beat additional 2 minutes. Bake in two 8-inch round layer pans at 375° oven for 25 to 35 minutes. Frost with chocolate frosting.

Toasted Pecan Cake

1 cup butter
2 cups sugar
4 ounces cream cheese
4 egg yolks
½ cup water
½ t. vanilla flavoring
1 cup buttermilk
½ t. salt
2½ cups all-purpose flour
1 t. baking soda

4 egg whites, stiffly beaten

Cream butter, sugar, and cream cheese together; add egg yolks, flavoring, water, and buttermilk. Sift all dry ingredients together and add to mixture. Fold in egg whites, beaten. Bake in 8-inch pans, lined in bottom with waxed paper (after greasing and flouring) at 350° for 30 to 40 minutes. Makes a very moist cake.

Frosting:

1 stick butter
4 ounces cream cheese
1 pound confectioners' sugar
1½ cups pecans, chopped coarsely

Cream together butter, cream cheese, and confectioners' sugar. Add just enough milk to make the frosting mixture creamy. 1 or 2 tablespoons depending on how creamy you desire frosting. Brown pecans in butter. Frost between layers and sprinkle with browned nuts. Frost side of cake and put remaining nuts on top of cake.

When you dream, dream big.

Applesauce Cake

1½ cups applesauce (1 can)
2 T. cocoa
1 cup sugar
1 cup raisins
½ cup shortening, melted
2 cups flour
1 t. cinnamon
½ t. cloves
½ t. allspice
½ t. salt
2 t. soda

Put sugar, raisins, spices, salt, and cocoa in applesauce. Stir well. Add melted shortening, then flour which has been sifted with the soda. Bake in 8-inch square pan at 350° for one hour, or until done.

In every living thing is the spirit to be free.

Old-fashioned Peach Cake
(Makes 16 to 20 servings)

1 package yellow cake mix
1 1-pound 5-ounce can peach pie filling
3 eggs
½ t. lemon extract
½ cup chopped nuts

Topping:

½ cup sugar
½ cup flour
¼ cup (½ stick) butter or margarine, softened
½ t. lemon extract

Preheat oven to 350°. In a large bowl combine dry cake mix, pie filling, eggs, ½ teaspoon extract and nuts. Blend at low speed until completely moistened, about 1 minute. Beat 2 minutes at medium speed. Spread batter in a greased and floured 13x9x2-inch pan.

Topping: In a medium bowl combine the sugar, flour, softened butter and ½ teaspoon extract with a fork or pastry blender. (Mixture will be crumbly.) Sprinkle evenly over batter. Bake at 350° for 40-45 minutes until center springs back when touched lightly.

Cherry-topped Cheesecake

1 package yellow cake mix
2 T. oil
2 8-ounce packages cream cheese, softened
½ cup sugar
4 eggs
1½ cups milk
3 T. lemon juice
3 t. vanilla
1 21-ounce can cherry pie filling

Preheat oven to 300°. Reserve 1 cup of dry cake mix. In large mixing bowl combine remaining cake mix, 1 egg, and oil (mixture will be crumbly). Press this crust evenly into bottom and ¾ way up the sides of a greased 13x9-inch pan. In same bowl, blend cream cheese and sugar. Add 3 eggs and reserved cake mix. Beat 1 minute at medium speed. At low speed, slowly add milk and flavorings. Mix until smooth. Pour into crust. Bake at 300° for 45-55 minutes until center is firm. When cool, top with pie filling. Chill before serving. Can also be made and baked in two 9-inch pans for 40-50 minutes in 350° oven.

Dump Cake

½ box white cake mix (2 cups)
½ cup margarine
1 small can crushed pineapple, drained
1 can cherry pie filling
½ cup nuts

Put pineapple, pie filling, and nuts into a shallow 2-quart baking dish. Sprinkle with cake mix and dot with butter. Bake at 350° for 50 minutes or until crusty and golden. 1 cup coconut and 1 cup chopped nuts may also be added.

O Lord, help my words to be gracious and tender today, for tomorrow I may have to eat them.

"Old Testament" Cake
(RSV)

½ cup Psalm 55:21
1 cup Jeremiah 6:20
3 Isaiah 10:14
3 T. 1 Samuel 14:25
½ t. Leviticus 2:13
2 cups 1 Kings 4:22
2 t. Amos 4:5
2 t. 2 Chronicles 9:9
  (1 t. each cinnamon and nutmeg)
½ cup Judges 4:19
1 cup Nahum 3:12 (chopped)
1 cup Numbers 17:8 (sliced)
1 cup 2 Samuel 6:19

Cream butter and sugar. Add honey and beaten egg yolks. Add remaining dry ingredients, mixed alternately with milk. Stir in fruit and nuts. Fold in beaten egg whites last. Bake at 325° for about 45 minutes in a 9x13-inch pan. Serve with whipped cream topping.

In case you don't have time to look up the scriptures they are:

Psalm 55:21—**oil (butter)**
Jeremiah 6:20—**sweet cane (sugar)**
Isaiah 10:14—**eggs**
1 Samuel 14:25—**honey**
Leviticus 2:13—**salt**
1 Kings 4:22—**flour**
Amos 4:5—**leavening (baking powder)**
2 Chronicles 9:9—**spices**
Judges 4:19—**milk**
Nahum 3:12—**figs**
Numbers 17:8—**almonds**
2 Samuel 6:19—**raisins**

Fresh Apple Cake

2 cups sugar
1½ cups liquid shortening
3 cups flour
1 t. cinnamon
3 cups diced apples
1 cup chopped nuts
1 t. almond extract
2 beaten eggs
1 t. soda
1 t. salt

Combine sugar, shortening, eggs, and flavoring. Sift together dry ingredients; blend into first mixture. Fold in apples and nuts. Grease and flour oblong cake pan. Bake 45 minutes at 350°.

For those who believe, no proof is necessary.

Broiled Sugar Coconut Cake

1 cup brown sugar
½ cup butter
2 eggs, well beaten
½ t. cloves
1 t. cinnamon
2 cups whole wheat flour
1 cup sour cream
1 t. baking soda
½ cup applesauce
1 cup raisins

1. *Cream sugar and butter.*
2. *Add eggs and mix well.*
3. *Sift flour and spices.*
4. *Mix raisins into flour mixture.*
5. *Mix soda with sour cream.*
6. *Add flour mixture, sour cream and applesauce to creamed mixture. Beat well.*
7. *Bake 30 minutes at 350°. Use an 8x11-inch pan.*

During baking period, prepare icing as follows:

¼ cup butter
¾ cup brown sugar
1 cup shredded coconut

Melt butter; add sugar and coconut. After cake has baked, pull oven rack out enough to permit room to spread icing over cake. Return cake to oven and turn on broiler to allow icing to sizzle for about 3 minutes.

Apple Kuchen

¾ cup butter
¾ cup sugar
2 eggs
1 t. grated lemon rind
1½ cups flour
1 t. baking powder
½ t. salt
¼ cup milk
3 to 4 medium apples, pared and cored
2 T. flour
1 t. cinnamon

Cream ½ cup butter and ¼ cup sugar until light and fluffy. Beat in eggs and rind. Combine 1¼ cups flour, baking powder, and salt. Add alternately with milk to creamed mixture, beating smooth after each addition. Spread in buttered 11x7x1½-inch baking dish. Slice the apples thinly. Arrange in rows on the batter. Combine ½ cup sugar, flour, and cinnamon; cut in ¼ cup butter as for pie crust. Sprinkle over apples. Bake at 375° 20 to 25 minutes, depending upon apples. Apples should be tender and golden brown. Serve slightly warm. Try ice cream or whipped cream on top.

Banana Cake

1½ cups sugar
⅔ cup shortening
2 eggs
1 cup mashed bananas
½ t. salt
5 T. buttermilk
1 t. vanilla
2 cups flour
1 t. soda
1 t. baking powder

Cream sugar and shortening; add slightly beaten eggs. Sift dry ingredients and add alternately with milk. Add bananas and blend. Bake in round, greased and floured pans at 350°.

Topping: *Prepare while cake is baking. Cook to the consistency of caramel: 10 tablespoons brown sugar, 6 tablespoons melted butter, and ¼ cup milk. Remove from heat and add 1 cup of nutmeats and 1 cup coconut. Spread on cake while cake is hot. Place under broiler until topping bubbles.*

Ideas don't work unless we do.

Texas Cake

2 sticks margarine
1 cup water
3 T. cocoa

Bring the above to a boil and pour over:

2 cups flour
2 cups sugar
½ t. salt

Mix well and add:

2 eggs (well beaten)
1 t. soda
½ cup buttermilk
1 t. vanilla
1 t. cinnamon

Bake in a greased cookie sheet or jelly roll pan 20 minutes at 350°

Frosting:

1 stick margarine
3 T. cocoa
6 T. milk
1 one pound box powdered sugar
½ cup pecans, chopped
1 t. vanilla

Heat the above ingredients, but do not boil. Pour over the cake.

Mississippi Mud Cake

1 cup (2 sticks) butter
⅓ cup cocoa
4 eggs
2 cups sugar
1½ cups flour
¼ t. salt
1½ cups chopped nuts
1 7-ounce jar marshmallow creme or 2
   cups miniature marshmallows

Melt butter; stir in cocoa. Add eggs, sugar, flour, and salt to melted mixture; mix well. Stir in nuts. Pour into a greased 11x14-inch pan or two 8-inch square pans. Bake at 350° for 30 minutes.

When done spread with marshmallow creme or marshmallows and return to oven, if necessary, to melt topping. Cool cake. Frost with following icing.

Icing

½ cup butter (1 stick)
⅓ cup cocoa
⅓ cup milk
1 one pound box confectioners' sugar
1 t. vanilla

Melt butter and cocoa; add milk and bring to a boil; boil one minute. Add sugar and vanilla. Beat until smooth. Frost cooled cake.

Old Southern Ice Box Coconut Cake

Overnight soak:

2 cups sour cream
2 cups white sugar
3 6-ounce packages frozen coconut or
   2 cans

Next day

Bake two-layer yellow cake mix. Cool. Cut in 4 layers. Put sour cream mixture between layers and on top. Leave in refrigerator at least one day before serving—preferably 3 days (covered).

Boston Cream Pie

There are many ways you can make this delicious cake. Use your favorite yellow cake recipe or use a mix. Bake (using only one 9-inch layer) and after cooled, split and fill middle with a custard cream pudding (either made from scratch or a box mix). Frost with a shiny chocolate frosting or sprinkle with confectioners' sugar. Delicious!

Pineapple Upside-Down Cake

¼ cup margarine
½ cup brown sugar
3 eggs, beaten
1 cup sugar
½ cup pineapple juice
1 t. vanilla
1½ cups flour
1 t. baking powder
pineapple slices
cherries

Melt margarine and brown sugar in iron frying pan. Beat eggs until light. Add 1 cup sugar, ½ cup pineapple juice, and vanilla. Add flour and baking powder.

Place pineapple slices in brown sugar mixture. Pour batter over all. Bake for 25 to 30 minutes at 350°. Cherries can be placed inside pineapple slices before or after baking.

Chocolate Cupcakes
Makes about 3 dozen

1 8-ounce package softened cream cheese
1 egg
⅓ cup sugar
⅛ t. salt

Cream the above ingredients together. Then add one 6-ounce package mini-chocolate chips.

3 cups flour
2 cups sugar
½ cup cocoa
2 t. baking soda
2 t. baking powder
1 t. salt

Sift together in a large bowl.

2 cups water
⅔ cup oil
2 t. white vinegar
2 t. vanilla

Add to the above flour mixture. Fill paper cupcake holders about ½ full. Drop a teaspoon of the chip mixture in each cupcake. Bake at 400° for 10 to 15 minutes.

Lazy Daisy Cake

1 T. margarine
½ cup milk
2 eggs
1 cup sugar
1 cup flour
¼ t. baking powder
1 t. baking powder

Heat together the margarine and milk. Set aside. Combine 2 eggs and 1 cup sugar; beat well. Sift together the flour and ¼ teaspoon baking powder, and add to eggs and sugar. Mix well, then add hot milk and margarine gradually. Put in 1 teaspoon baking powder last. Bake in 325° oven about 35 minutes. Use 8x12-inch pan.

Topping: *Melt together 3 tablespoons butter, 5 tablespoons brown sugar, 2 tablespoons cream. Add ¾ cup coconut. When cake is done, spread this on top while it is hot; place under broiler to toast. Watch carefully, for it burns easily.*

Old Witch's Magic Nut Cake

3 eggs
1 pound can of pumpkin
¾ cup vegetable oil

Beat together and then add:

2½ cups flour
2¼ cups sugar
1½ t. baking soda
¾ t. nutmeg
¾ t. cinnamon
1 cup yellow raisins
½ cup chopped walnuts

Pour into a loaf pan or 2 greased round pans. Bake at 350° for 35 minutes or until done.

Frost with:

3 ounces cream cheese
4 T. butter
1 t. lemon juice or vanilla extract
½ box confectioners' sugar

Sprinkle with chopped nuts.

Fruitcake

2½ cups flour
2 t. baking powder
2 pounds dates (cut in thirds)
1 pound whole candied cherries—half red and half green
1 pound candied pineapple (broken into pieces)
2 pounds whole pecan halves
8 eggs beaten
1 t. salt
3 T. vanilla
1½ cups sugar

Mix the flour, salt, and baking powder in a large bowl. Add the fruit mixture coating it well with the flour. Add the eggs and the rest of the ingredients. Line six 1-pound cans (or 10-12 smaller ones) with brown paper that has been greased. Place a pan of water in the bottom of the oven and bake at 300° for 80 minutes or until fruitcake is done. Store in a closed container.

Pray as though no work would help, and work as though no prayer would help.

Carrot Cake

2 cups flour
2 cups sugar
2 t. cinnamon
2 t. soda
½ t. salt
4 eggs
1½ cups salad oil
3 cups shredded carrots

Frosting:

1 pound powdered sugar
8 ounce package cream cheese
1 stick butter
2 t. vanilla

For cake, simply mix all ingredients in a large bowl with an electric mixer. No sifting needed. Bake in a greased 9x13-inch pan for 40-45 minutes at 350°.

Cool cake and top with frosting. Make frosting by creaming together cheese and butter and vanilla then adding powdered sugar.

Sour Cream Pound Cake

3 cups sugar
2 sticks butter
6 eggs
3 cups flour
¼ t. soda
1 cup sour cream
1 t. vanilla

Cream together sugar and butter. Add eggs one at a time and beat. Add flour, soda, sour cream, and vanilla alternately to mixture until combined. Bake in greased and floured pans: Angel food cake pan—1½ hours. 2 loaf pans—¾-1 hour. Bake at 350°. Top with ice cream, fruit, whipped cream, and so on.

Dream Cake

1 package, 2-layer size, yellow, white, or devil's food cake mix.
1 envelope whipped topping mix. (Do not whip: use right from envelope.)
4 eggs
1 cup cold tap water.

Combine all ingredients in large bowl of electric mixer. Blend until moistened. Beat at medium speed for 4 minutes. Pour into two greased and floured 9-inch layer pans, and bake at 350° for 30 minutes. Cool cakes for 10 minutes in the pans. Remove from pans; finish cooling on cake racks. Frost, sprinkle with confectioners' sugar, or top with fruit, syrup, or ice cream.

A Dream Cake can be baked in other size pans, as well:

in three 8-inch layer pans, bake for 35 minutes;

in one 13x9-inch pan, bake for 40 to 45 minutes;

in cupcake pans, bake for about 20 minutes;

in one 10-inch tube pan, bake for 45 to 50 minutes (cool for 15 minutes).

For altitudes above 3,500 feet: Prepare Dream Cake as directed, adding 2 tablespoons flour, using a total of 1 cup plus 3 tablespoons water and baking at 375° for about 5 minutes less or until cake tests done.

You can fly, but you must get out of the cocoon.

Amish Cake

2 cups flour
1½ cups sugar
2 t. soda
1 t. salt
2 eggs, beaten
1 t. vanilla
1 pound can crushed pineapple with
   juice
½ cup nuts

Mix all together and bake in 9x13-inch ungreased pan for 40-45 minutes in 350° oven.

Frosting

2 3-ounce packages cream cheese
½ cup powdered sugar
1 t. vanilla
¼ cup butter

Blend cream cheese and butter together. Add powdered sugar. Then add vanilla. Spread on cooled cake.

Beware of despairing about yourself; you are commanded to put your trust in God, not yourself.

Rhubarb Cake

½ cup shortening
1½ cups light brown sugar
1 egg well beaten
1 t. vanilla
1½ cups finely cut rhubarb
1 cup sour milk or 2 T. vinegar added
   to sweet milk to make 1 cup
2 cups flour
1 t. soda
½ t. salt

Cream shortening and brown sugar together; add beaten egg and vanilla. Mix alternately milk and sifted dry ingredients to the first mixture. Add rhubarb. Before baking top with a mixture of ¼ cup white sugar and ½ teaspoon cinnamon. Bake at 350° for 45 minutes.

Strawberry Whip Cake Topping

1 cup granulated sugar
1 egg white
½ to 1 cup strawberries

Place all ingredients in bowl and beat for several minutes or until stiff. Spread on sheet cake and top with whole berries.

Creamy Caramel Icing

For Large cake:

⅓ cup cream
6 T. butter
2 T. sugar
3 cups confectioners' sugar

For small cake:

¼ cup cream
4½ T. butter
2 T. sugar
2¼ cups confectioners' sugar

Heat together cream and butter. Meanwhile caramelize 2 tablespoons sugar. Add scalded cream and butter, stirring until lumps are dissolved. Gradually stir in confectioners' sugar. Beat until smooth, creamy, and right to spread. Add more cream if too thick.

Burnt Sugar Icing

2 cups white sugar
1 cup cream (don't use canned milk)
2 T. white sugar
¼ cup butter
pinch of salt

Put 2 cups sugar and cream in pan and let come to a boil. Burn 2 tablespoons white sugar in skillet or pan and stir, while pouring, into other mixture. Let come to a boil to 245°. Add butter after removing from fire; pinch of salt.

60-Second Icing

1 cup semisweet chocolate pieces
¼ cup butter
½ cup canned milk
1½ cups confectioners' sugar

Melt chocolate and butter together; allow to cool; blend in sugar with milk. Beat briskly.

Life is not the wick or the candle—it is the burning.

Parents and elementary school teachers share one of life's special joys—that of hearing the events of the world interpreted by children. Children's expressions represent the young speakers' points of view and, while humorous to us as adults, are spoken in all sincerity.

For example, some first graders responded to my pregnancy in these terms:

"I don't think you should jump rope. It makes the baby dizzy."

"Is your husband getting fatter, too?"

"Since the baby won't come until I'm in second grade, I guess it's still in the egg."

"My mom had a baby once."

Or consider the insights of this third grader questioning me.

"Where do you work?" she asked. A bit taken aback, I explained that my job was that of teaching children.

Still not satisfied, the child replied incredulously, "You mean you get *paid* for doing this?"

And don't forget children's perceptiveness—even in such adult areas as dialects and accents.

I moved from the Midwest, and had just started teaching in the East when I overheard two of my pupils playing school.

"I get to be the teacher," said one.

"Okay, but you have to talk funny like she does," replied the other.

When I was visiting friends in the South, I had a T-shirt on with YALE printed across the front. Five-year-old Alison asked what it said and when I replied "Yale" she immediately started to jump up and down and yell.

"What are you doing, Alison?" I asked.

"Well, you told me to 'Yale' didn't you?"

Oh, the joy that children bring to our lives!

CANDY

OTHER SWEETS

Candy

Texas Pecan Candy
Makes about 2½ dozen

1 pound light brown sugar
2 T. light corn syrup
¼ cup butter or margarine
1 t. vanilla
1½ cups coarsely chopped pecans

In medium saucepan over medium heat, cook sugar, ⅓ cup water, and corn syrup until boiling, stirring constantly; continue cooking and stirring until temperature reaches 238° on a candy thermometer or until mixture dropped in cold water forms a small soft ball. Remove from the heat and add the butter or margarine, but do not stir. Cool to lukewarm or 110°.

With spoon beat in vanilla until mixture is thickened and semiglossy. Stir in pecans. Quickly drop by rounded teaspoonfuls onto waxed paper. Spread drops into small circles. Let stand until the candies are firm and sugared.

Caramel Snappers
Makes 18

72 pecan halves or about 1 cup
36 caramels
2 1-ounce squares candy baking chocolate, melted

Grease baking sheet; on it arrange pecans, flat side down, in groups of 4. Place 2 caramels on each cluster of pecans. Heat in slow oven at 325°, until caramels soften, about 8 minutes. Remove from oven; with a buttered spatula, flatten caramels over pecans. Cool; remove from pan to waxed paper. Brush tops with melted chocolate.

Cream Cheese Chocolate Fudge

1 3-ounce package cream cheese
2 cups sifted confectioners' sugar
2 1-ounce squares of unsweetened chocolate, melted
¼ t. vanilla
dash of salt
½ cup chopped pecans

Place the cream cheese in a bowl; cream it until soft and smooth. Slowly blend the sugar into it. Add the melted chocolate. Mix well. Add vanilla, salt and chopped pecans and mix until well blended. Press into a well-greased, shallow pan. Place in refrigerator until firm for about 15 minutes. Cut into squares. For slightly softer fudge blend in 1 teaspoon of cream.

When all is said and done there's a lot more said than done.

Foolproof Fudge
Makes about 2 pounds

⅔ cup or small can undiluted evaporated milk
1⅔ cup sugar
½ t. salt
½ cup chopped nuts
1½ cups diced marshmallows (about 16 medium) or may use 1 cup marshmallow creme
1½ cups chocolate chips
1 t. vanilla

Mix milk, sugar, and salt in saucepan over low heat. Heat to boiling; then cook 5 minutes, stirring constantly. Remove from heat. Add nuts, marshmallows, chocolate, and vanilla. Stir 1 to 2 minutes, until marshmallow is melted. Pour into buttered 9-inch square pan. Cool and cut into squares.

Date Pudding Candy

3 cups white sugar
1 cup evaporated milk
2 T. white corn syrup
pinch salt
1 large package dates

Add all together and cook to 232°. Add a lump of butter the size of a walnut. When cool add a cup of chopped pecans and beat until creamy. Pour into buttered 9x13-inch pan.

Peanut Butter Fudge

2 cups sugar
2/3 cup milk
1 cup marshmallow creme
1 cup chunk-style peanut butter
1 6-ounce package or 1 cup semisweet
    chocolate pieces
1 t. vanilla

Combine sugar and milk. Heat and stir over medium heat until sugar dissolves and mixture comes to boiling. Cook to 234° (soft-ball stage). Remove from heat; add remaining ingredients and stir well. Pour into 9x9-inch buttered pan. Score in squares while warm; cut when firm.

Honey-Sugared Walnuts

2½ cups walnut halves
1½ cups sugar
½ cup water
¼ cup honey
½ t. salt
½ t. cinnamon
½ t. vanilla

Toast walnuts in moderate oven at 375° for ten minutes, stirring once. Combine sugar, water, honey, salt, and cinnamon in pan and cook to soft-ball stage or 236°. Remove from heat and beat until mixture begins to get creamy. Add vanilla and warm nuts; stir gently until nuts are well coated and mixture becomes thick. Turn out on buttered baking sheet and with two forks separate the nuts at once.

Caramel Corn

2 cups brown sugar
1 cup white sugar
½ cup white Karo syrup
½ cup cold water
½ cup butter

Cook slowly until sugar is dissolved. Boil rapidly until mixture forms a hard ball in cold water. Pour over a dishpan full of salted popcorn.

White Fudge

Makes 1½ pounds

2¼ cups granulated sugar
½ cup dairy sour cream
¼ cup milk
2 T. butter
1 T. light corn syrup
¼ t. salt
2 t. vanilla
1 cup coarsely chopped Walnuts
⅓ cup quartered candied cherries

Combine sugar, sour cream, milk, butter, corn syrup and salt in heavy 2-quart saucepan. Stir over moderate heat until sugar is dissolved and mixture reaches a boil. Boil over moderate heat 9 to 10 minutes to 238° (240° if weather is damp) or soft ball stage. Remove from heat and allow to stand until lukewarm (110°), about 1 hour. Add vanilla, and beat until mixture just begins to lose its gloss and hold its shape. (Requires very little beating.) Quickly stir in walnuts and cherries, and turn into oiled pan. Let stand until firm before cutting.

Coconut Peaks

Makes about 3 dozen.

¼ cup butter or margarine
2 cups sifted powdered sugar
3 cups flaked coconut
¼ cup light cream
1 6-ounce package chocolate chips
2 t. shortening

In saucepan slowly heat butter or margarine till golden brown; gradually stir in powdered sugar, flaked coconut, and light cream. Drop by teaspoonfuls onto waxed paper. Refrigerate until easy to handle, then shape into peaks. Over hot, not boiling, water, melt chocolate pieces and shortening. Stir until smooth. Dip bottoms of the peaks into the melted chocolate mixture, then harden on a rack covered with waxed paper.

Hawaiian Panocha

1 cup granulated sugar
½ cup brown sugar
dash salt
¼ cup light cream
½ cup well-drained, crushed pineapple
1 T. butter
½ t. vanilla
walnut halves

Combine sugars, salt, cream, and pineapple. Stir to dissolve sugar. Heat to boiling. Cook to soft-ball stage at 236°; stir occasionally. Remove from heat. Add butter or fortified margarine. Cool to luke warm at 110° without stirring. Add vanilla. Beat until thick. Spread quickly into greased 6-inch square pan. Top with walnut halves.

Candy Buckeyes

½ pound butter
1 pound peanut butter
1½ pound powdered sugar
1 large package chocolate chips
½ cake paraffin

Soften butter; work in peanut butter and sugar. Form into balls the size of small buckeyes (chestnuts).

Melt in double boiler over hot water the chocolate and paraffin. Dip balls into hot chocolate, leaving bare spot to resemble buckeye. Use a 2- or 3-tined fork to dip buckeyes. Usually, there is enough chocolate to dip twice. Keep refrigerated.

Hard Candy

3¾ cups white sugar
1½ cups white Karo syrup
1 cup water
1 dram oil of any flavor
food coloring

Stir and boil the above ingredients until 300° on a candy thermometer. Take off the heat and stir in the color and dram of oil. Have ready 3 or 4 cookie sheets sprinkled with powdered sugar. Make "rivers" with your fingers in the sugar. Pour candy in the rivers. Let cool and break into pieces.

Quick Walnut Penuche

Makes 32 pieces.

½ cup butter or margarine
1 cup packed brown sugar
¼ cup milk
1¾ to 2 cups sifted powdered sugar
1 cup chopped walnuts

In saucepan melt butter. Stir in brown sugar. Cook and stir over low heat for 2 minutes. Add milk; bring to boiling. Cool to room temperature. Beat in powdered sugar till like fudge. Stir in nuts; pour in buttered 8x8x2-inch pan. Chill till firm enough to cut.

Marshmallow Pops

Makes 30 pops.

1. *Insert toothpick deep into each marshmallow (about 30 large marshmallows) and freeze.*

2. *Over hot (not boiling water melt 1 package (1 cup) butterscotch, milk chocolate, or semi-sweet chocolate morsels and 1 tablespoon shortening.*

3. *Coat each marshmallow with chocolate. Then roll in any of the following toppings: shredded coconut, chopped nuts, corn flake crumbs, graham cracker crumbs, colored cereal flakes, fruit flavored cereals, nonpareils, or gum drops. Set each pop in a colored cupcake liner. Chill till firm (about 20 minutes).*

Butter Pecan Torte

Serves 12-15

1 cup graham cracker crumbs
1 cup soda cracker crumbs
½ cup butter or margarine

Mix together and press into a 9x13x2-inch pan. Bake at 350° for 10 min. Cool.

2 3¾-ounce packages vanilla instant
   pudding
1 cup milk
1 quart softened butter pecan ice
   cream.

Mix the above ingredients together and put on top of the crust. Top with a whipped topping mix to which a little vanilla has been added. Crush 3 Heath candy bars and sprinkle on top. Refrigerate 6 to 8 hours. This can be made ahead. Hint: The candy bars will crush much easier if they are frozen.

Pumpkin Nut Torte

Serves 6

1 cup packed brown sugar
½ cup butter, softened
3 eggs
1½ cups crushed cinnamon-flavored
   graham crackers
1 t. baking powder
1 cup shredded coconut
1 cup chopped nuts
½ cup prepared pumpkin
½ pint whipping cream
3 T. sugar
½ t. cinnamon
¼ t. nutmeg

Cream sugar and butter. Beat in eggs one at a time. Stir in crumbs and baking powder. Stir in coconut, nuts, and pumpkin. Spread in greased and floured 9-inch square pan. Bake at 325° 35 to 40 minutes.

Cool completely. Cut into six pieces. Meanwhile whip cream with sugar and spices. Spoon onto each serving.

Mandarin Ginger Torte

1 14½-ounce package gingerbread mix
1 cup heavy cream
1 cup marshmallow creme
1 11-ounce can mandarin orange
   segments (drained)

Prepare gingerbread according to directions using an 8-inch layer pan. Cool, then cut the cake in half. Whip the cream until slightly thickened. Add the marshmallow creme to the whipped cream mixture, beating until stiff. Fold the oranges into the cream mixture. Fill and top the gingerbread with the cream mixture.

Butterscotch Pudding Dessert
Serves 12-15

1 cup flour
1 stick melted margarine
½ cup chopped pecans

Mix these ingredients together, and pat the dough in the bottom of a 9x13x2-inch pan. Bake at 350° for 15 minutes.

1 8-ounce package softened cream
  cheese
1 cup confectioners' sugar
1 cup ready-made whipped topping

Blend these ingredients together and put to the side.

2 3¾-ounce packages butterscotch or
  chocolate pudding—not instant

Use only 3 cups of milk instead of what the package calls for. Cook until thick. Cool. Spread the cheese mixture on the baked crust. Put the pudding on top of the cheese mixture. Cover with a whipped topping and toasted coconut.

Brennan's Caramel Cup Custard
6 Servings

6 egg yolks
1 cup sugar
¼ t. salt
2 cups milk
½ t. vanilla
dash nutmeg

Beat together egg yolks, ½ cup sugar, salt, and nutmeg to mix. Scald milk and pour into egg mixture. Stir to blend. Stir in vanilla. In a small iron skillet, caramelize the other ½ cup sugar. Pour a little into each of 6 custard cups. When caramel sets, pour custard mixture into cups. Set cups in pan of hot water 1 inch deep. Bake in preheated oven 350° 45 to 50 minutes or until silver knife inserted 1 inch from edge comes out clean. Quickly remove from heat and allow to cool. Unmold and serve.

I am not bound to win, but I am bound to be true.

—Abraham Lincoln

Coconut Ice Cream Balls with Hot Fudge Sauce

12 ice cream balls (vanilla)
1 package coconut

Toast the coconut in the oven. Watch it carefully as it burns easily. Bake at 325° for about 10 minutes. Roll the ice cream balls in the coconut and put on a tray in the freezer.

Hot Fudge Sauce

1 cup milk
1½ 1-ounce squares unsweetened chocolate
1 cup sugar
2 T. light corn syrup
dash of salt
1 t. vanilla
2 T. butter

In a saucepan combine milk and chocolate; cook over low heat, stirring occasionally, until chocolate is melted. Stir in sugar, corn syrup, and salt; bring to a boil over medium heat, stirring occasionally. Simmer for 5 minutes. Remove from heat and stir in vanilla and butter. Serve hot over coconut ice cream balls.

Banana Split Dessert

½ cup margarine, melted
2 cups crushed graham cracker crumbs
2 eggs
2 cups sifted powdered sugar
¾ cup margarine, softened
2 t. vanilla
1 20-ounce can crushed pineapple in heavy syrup, well drained
4 medium bananas, sliced
1 9-ounce carton whipped topping
½ cup chopped nuts
1 small jar maraschino cherries (drained and chopped)

Combine ½ cup melted margarine and crumbs. Put in 9x13-inch pan. Beat eggs at high speed until light and fluffy.

Add powdered sugar, softened butter and vanilla, beat for five minutes and then spread over crumb mixture. Chill for 30 minutes. Spread pineapple over cream mixture. Place banana slices on top of pineapple. Cover with whipped topping and decorate with cherries and nuts. Refrigerate at least six hours or overnight.

Thanks, God. I really like the day you made today.

Apple Dessert

6 Washington apples
½ cup water
½ t. cinnamon
2 t. shredded lemon peel
1 cup brown sugar, firmly packed
¾ cup Grapenuts
6 T. butter or margarine
6 T flour

Core and thinly slice the unpared apples. Arrange overlapping slices in shallow, buttered 1½-quart baking dish. Pour water over apples, then sprinkle with cinnamon and shredded lemon peel. Mix sugar, Grapenuts, butter, and flour until crumbly. Cover apples with mixture. Bake at 350° about 45 minutes, or until apples are tender and crust is nicely browned. Serve warm or cold with cream.

Apple Fritters

1 egg, separated
⅓ cup milk
½ cup flour
2 t. sugar
¼ t. salt
½ t. baking powder
2 t. cooking oil
2 tart apples
powdered sugar

Beat egg yolk until light. Combine with milk. Mix flour with sugar, salt, and baking powder. Sift twice and stir into egg and milk. Beat until smooth. Stir in 2 teaspoons cooking oil. Fold in stiffly beaten egg white. Cover. Let stand 30 minutes. Peel, quarter, and slice thin 2 tart apples. Stir into mixture and drop from spoon into hot fat. Drain on soft paper. Serve hot with powdered sugar.

Apple Crisp
Makes 15 servings

6 to 8 cups sliced apples
1 cup sugar
1 cup rolled oats
½ cup flour
1 t. cinnamon
½ cup or 1 stick butter, melted

Place sliced apples in bottom of greased 13x9-inch baking dish. Combine sugar, oats, flour, and cinnamon; mix in melted butter. Sprinkle over apples. Bake at 375° for 1 hour. Serve warm.

The plum tree suggests courage, because it puts out its blossoms while the snow is on the ground.

Fruit Kabobs

Use wooden skewers (usually bamboo) which may be purchased at most department or china stores. They are fun to use!

Use your imagination as you fill them with fruits. Chunks of watermellon, cantaloupe, honeydew, pineapple, mandarin oranges, peaches are some that may be used. For banana chunks roll them in sour cream which has been thinned with just a little lemon juice. Then as an elegant topping, roll it again in flaked coconut.

This makes a beautiful dessert or appetizer. Arrange as many as you need for your number of guests on a large plate and then sit back and wait for the compliments.

Scalloped Pineapple

1 large can crushed pineapple
1 stick butter or margarine
1 cup sugar
4 slices bread, cubed, with crusts
   removed

Mix all ingredients, including syrup from the pineapple, together and put in a baking dish. Bake at 350° for 30 minutes.

Indian Pudding

2 cups corn bread crumbs
4 cups milk
2 eggs, lightly beaten
⅔ cup maple syrup
½ t. cinnamon
¼ t. ginger
½ t. salt
1 T. melted butter

Preheat oven to 350°. Grease a 2-quart casserole. Combine corn bread crumbs and milk and let stand 10 minutes. Beat in eggs, syrup, spices, and salt. Stir in butter. Pour into casserole. Bake 1½ hours. After the first 30 minutes of baking, slide a spoon under top crust and stir pudding gently without stirring crust into pudding. Serve warm or cold with whipped cream or ice cream.

Strawberry Supreme

Serves 12

½ cup butter
1 cup flour
¼ cup brown sugar
½ cup nuts

Mix the above ingredients together and bake on a cookie sheet for 15 minutes at 400°, stirring often. Divide in half and put to the side.

Put half of the topping mixture in a 9x13x2-inch pan.

1 package frozen strawberries
2 egg whites
1 cup sugar
1 T. lemon juice
1 t. vanilla

Beat the above ingredients for 15 to 20 minutes. Then add ½ pint whipped whipping cream. Pour over the top of the crumbly mixture and add the rest of the crumbs as a topping. Freeze overnight.

Old-Fashioned Strawberry Cake

2 cups all-purpose flour
1 T. sugar
3 t. baking powder
½ t. salt
⅓ cup butter or margarine
1 beaten egg
⅔ cup milk
3 to 4 cups sugared, sliced
  strawberries
1 cup whipped cream, whipped with a
  little confectioners' sugar added

Sift together dry ingredients; cut in butter till mixture is coarse like crumbs. Combine egg and milk stirring only until moist. Turn dough out on floured surface; knead gently for about one minute. Roll out to ½-inch thickness. Cut 6 biscuits with a floured 2½-inch round cutter. Bake on an ungreased baking sheet at 450° for 10 minutes. Split the biscuits and fill with the berries. Top the dessert with berries and whipped cream.

Cream Puffs

Makes 8 large cream puffs

¼ **cup shortening**
½ **cup boiling water**
½ **cup sifted enriched flour**
¼ **t. salt**
2 eggs

Combine shortening and boiling water. Stir over low heat until shortening is melted. Add flour and salt all at once and beat until ingredients are completely smooth. Remove from heat. Add eggs, one at a time, beating vigorously after each addition. Drop from tablespoon to baking sheet, slightly greased. Leave 2 inches between puffs to permit spreading.

Bake 10 minutes in hot oven at 450°. Lower temperature to 350° and continue baking 20 minutes longer. Puffs should be golden brown and crisp. When cold, cut off tops with a sharp knife. Fill with flavored whipped cream, ice cream, or a filling made from a pudding mix. Replace tops. May be topped with hot fudge.

Jesus said, "These things I have spoken to you, that my joy may be in you, and that your joy may be full" (John 15:11).

My joy—in you—that your joy—may be full. It seems to me that it is this quality of life that is so important—to be joyful, which is to be happy, which is to be thankful, which is to be grateful. I wrote the following in one of those moments when I was experiencing gratitude of my world through my senses. It was used as an insert in the church bulletin, and one little boy came up to me after church and said, "I love the smell of tomato plants, too."

There is work to do—my daily work that I am tied to in managing a home and raising a family. But summer is here and with it the sights and sounds of my world. My world is not the New England hills, glistening prairies, great mountains, or the sea. My world is my little Indiana backyard.

But today I shall not let duty blind my eyes or dull my senses to this—my world. I shall, like Moses "turn aside and see this great sight." Today, I shall pause and *choose* . . .

TO SEE
the scampering chipmunk and frisky rabbit,
the delicate blossom turn to fruit, and look at
the soothing colors of grass, sky, and clouds;

TO HEAR
the cooing of the doves,
the belligerent blue jay commands,
the gentle voices of my neighbors,
and
the busy traffic just a block away;
TO SMELL
the fresh green tomato plants,
the honeysuckle vine my folks gave to me, and
the smell of frying bacon;
TO TOUCH AND FEEL
the velvet petals of a hybrid rose,
the refreshing dew on my bare feet, and
the strong arms of my children.

Yes, I feel refreshed, renewed, and restored. I'm glad I took time to turn aside and see the wonder. I feel the magic of closeness and the warmth and tenderness of the moment. I feel alive to God and his world. My tensions drain away. And now—I go back to serving. Thank you, Lord.

As we look at the process of growing, we can look clear-eyed at reality and define, and then redefine the growing edge of ourselves. Growth in personality, maturity, and inner beauty gives us daily new beginnings. We look at the new dimensions of our life, decide to risk in order to attain the goals before us, and choose to develop to our full potential. Growing takes hard work, much as a plant. The soil, water, and sun work together with the cultivating, pruning, and developing. Then we watch the change and growth to fruition. But we must trust and not be too impatient. Remember the little boy who wanted to see if his plant was growing? Every night he pulled it up to look at the roots to see what was happening. Life is not a courtyard but much more like a laboratory where we are growing, experimenting, and making mistakes. Growth is an evidence of life.

We grow best if we have a caring group of five or six significant persons who will help us grow. These people will nurture, listen, understand, but not dominate or smother us; it is this small, supportive group who will enable us to survive and cope with the present moment brutalities of life. They are our "gardeners" who encourage, have faith in, and love us in spite of. Then the growing edge is fresh, new, and beautiful for the human spirit is meant for new beginnings. Perhaps the new beginning for you today is to determine that it is much more important to decide on the way you want to live than what you will be. A new thought, concept, or idea continues to stir within us and moves us toward that person that God wants us to be.

This is a weighty problem for about ten million of us in the United States. We have a land of too much food and our discipline is not equal to the occasion. Many people think that overeating gives them pleasure, but really the pleasure comes in eating what is right for them. A nagging sense of guilt accompanies reaching for the calorie-laden dessert. However, feeling and looking our best is reason enough for many to be food and food-content conscious. It is refreshing to see many young mothers carefully examining the contents of food products to see what additives, supplements, and preservatives they contain. It is good stewardship to remember that the calories do count. Our weight reflects the number of calories we take in minus the number of calories we burn up.

Our eating habits are almost as important as what it is we do eat. We are learning that eating, too quickly or in unpleasant surroundings, nibbling, or unconsciously eating when tense or depressed are patterns that may need to be changed in order for a diet to be effective. Our state of mind or our reasons for dieting can reinforce the stimulus for dieting.

By the way, have you noticed the kinds of diets that you can find in books and magazines? It is fantastically easy to find the kind of diet that will help you shed pounds "miraculously." For fun, here are some that I found:

Grapefruit diet - Milk diet - Skiers diet - 100 calorie diet - Water diet - Rice diet - Hot dog diet - Ten day, ten pounds off diet - Strawberry and cream diet - Diet of the month - Corrective diet for fatigued people - Psychologists' eat-anything diet - and on, and on, and on.

But the word of caution for any diet is to check with your doctor; be sensible and, as some of my friends would say, the best kind of diet is to "shut my mouth."

Hey, Diddle, Diddle, I'm watching my middle
   And hoping to whittle it soon,
      But eating's such fun,
      I may not get it done
Till my dish runs away with my spoon.
                              —Conrad Fiorello

40

Pies

Blueberry Cream Pie
Serves 8

1 package Dream Whip
½ cup cold milk
½ t. vanilla
1 3-ounce package creamed cheese
1½ cups powdered sugar
½ 21-ounce can blueberry pie filling
1 graham cracker crust

Whip one package Dream Whip with milk and vanilla according to package directions. Cream together the creamed cheese and powdered sugar. Mix with Dream Whip and pour into cooled graham cracker pie crust. Top with pie filling. Refrigerate. Let cream filling cool prior to topping with blueberries.

Butterscotch Pie

1½ cups brown sugar
1½ cups water
3 T. flour
3 T cornstarch
2 T white sugar
2 egg yolks
3 T. butter
⅛ t. salt
1 t. vanilla

Heat brown sugar and water to boiling point and pour over sifted flour, cornstarch, and white sugar. Cook until thick. Add slightly beaten egg yolks. Cook one minute longer. Remove from fire. Add butter, salt, and vanilla. Let cool, and pour into pie shell.

Old Fashioned Sugar Cream Pie

1 cup sugar
¼ cup cornstarch
2 cups milk

Cook until thick. Remove from stove. Add one stick of butter (or margarine) and one teaspoon vanilla.

Pour into a baked pie shell. Sprinkle with cinnamon. Bake at 350° for 15 minutes. Refrigerate.

Cream Pie

⅓ cup flour
⅔ cup sugar
¼ t. salt
2 cups milk, scalded
3 slightly beaten egg yolks
½ t. vanilla
1 9-inch baked shell
3 stiffly beaten egg whites
6 T. sugar
2 T. butter or margarine

Mix flour, ⅔ cup sugar, and salt; gradually add heated milk. Cook in double boiler until thick, stirring often. Add small amount to egg yolks; then pour back into remaining hot mixture and cook 2 minutes longer. Cool. Add butter and vanilla. Pour into baked shell and cover with meringue made of egg whites and 6 tablespoons sugar. Bake in moderate oven 350° about 12 minutes.

Banana Cream Pie

Makes 9-inch pie

9-inch baked pie shell
½ cup sugar
¼ t. salt
3 T. flour
1½ cups milk
2 eggs
1 t. butter
½ t. vanilla
1½ cups heavy cream, whipped
3 medium bananas, sliced

1. *Prepare pie shell.*
2. *In small bowl combine sugar, salt, and flour. Stir in ½ cup of the milk to make a smooth paste.*
3. *Put remaining milk in top of double saucepan; scald. Stir in paste; cook over hot water, stirring constantly, until thickened and smooth.*
4. *In small bowl beat eggs; stir in a little of hot mixture. Return to rest of hot mixture; cook over hot water, stirring constantly for 5 minutes.*
5. *Remove from heat; stir in butter and vanilla. Cool custard, stirring occasionally.*
6. *Fold in half the cream. Arrange half the bananas in pie shell; cover with half the custard. Top with remaining bananas; cover with remaining custard.*
7. *Spread remaining cream on top; refrigerate for at least one hour.*

Two things we give our children— roots and wings.

Streusel Cream Peach Pie

1 unbaked 9-inch pie shell
4 cups peeled and quartered peaches
   (8-10)
½ cup sugar
½ t. nutmeg
1 egg
2 t. half-and-half cream
¼ cup packed brown sugar
½ cup flour
¼ cup soft butter

Arrange peaches in shell. Combine sugar and nutmeg; sprinkle over peaches. Beat together the egg and half-and-half; pour over peaches and sugar. Mix brown sugar, flour, and butter together until crumbly. Sprinkle over top of pie. Bake at 425° for 35-45 minutes, or until lightly browned. Serve warm topped with whipped cream, sour cream, or ice cream.

Lemon Sponge Pie

3 T. shortening
⅛ t. salt
¾ cup sugar
2½ T. flour
2 egg whites, stiffly beaten
2 egg yolks
1 cup milk
juice and grated rind of 1 lemon

Combine shortening, salt, sugar, and flour. Mix well. Add egg yolks, milk, lemon juice, and rind. Beat with rotary beater until smooth. Fold in beaten egg whites. Pour in unbaked pie shell. Bake in moderate oven about 40 minutes, or until brown.

Pecan Pie

1 cup pecans
3 eggs
½ cup sugar
1 cup dark corn syrup
⅛ t. salt
¼ cup melted butter
1 t. vanilla

Combine butter and sugar. Add syrup, eggs, salt, and vanilla. Mix thoroughly and add coarsely broken nutmeats. Pour into unbaked pie shell. Bake at 425° for ten minutes, then at 400° about 40 minutes longer until custard is firm. Cool before serving.

There is no place like here.
There is no time like now.

Chess Pie

3 egg yolks
¾ cup sugar
½ cup butter or margarine, softened
3 T. heavy cream
generous dash of nutmeg
pinch of salt
1 unbaked 8-inch pie shell

Beat egg yolks until thick and lemon-colored. Beat in sugar, butter, cream, nutmeg, and salt. Pour into pie shell. Bake in preheated 350° oven 30 to 35 minutes, until filling is set at edges but still soft.

Perfect Apple Pie

6 or 7 tart apples
1 cup sugar
2 T. flour
1 t. cinnamon
dash nutmeg
dash salt
pastry for 2-crust 9-inch pie
2 T. butter or margarine

Pare apples and slice thin. Combine flour, sugar, spices, and salt; mix with apples. Line a 9-inch pie plate with pastry, fill with apple mixture and dot with butter or margarine. Place top crust on, sprinkle with sugar if desired. Bake at 400° for about 50 minutes or until done.

White Christmas Pie

Mix and set aside:

¼ cup cold water and 1 T. gelatin

Place in saucepan:

½ cup sugar
2 T. flour
½ t. salt
3 egg yolks, slightly beaten
1½ cup milk

Cook over low heat until it boils, stirring constantly. Boil 1 minute. Remove from stove and add gelatin. Cool. When starting to set, fold in:

¾ T. vanilla
¼ t. almond extract
3 egg whites, stiffly beaten with
½ cup sugar and ¼ t. cream of tartar

Fold in:

½ cup cream, whipped
1 cup moist coconut

Pour in baked pie shell. Refrigerate and serve with thin layer of whipped cream.

Custard Pie

Plain pastry for one 9-inch pie:

1 cup sifted flour
⅓ cup shortening
1 t. salt
4 to 5 T. cold water

Cut shortening into salt and flour mixture. Sprinkle water, tablespoon at a time, over mixture. Mix with fork; pour onto waxed paper and form into ball. Let stand a few minutes. Flatten slightly and roll on lightly floured pastry cloth. Roll dough and fit 9-inch shell.

Filling:

4 slightly beaten eggs
½ cup sugar
¼ t. salt
½ t. vanilla
½ t. almond extract
2½ cups scalded milk
nutmeg

Blend eggs, sugar, salt, vanilla, and almond extract. Gradually stir in scalded milk. Pour into chilled unbaked pie shell. Bake at 400° for 25 to 30 minutes. Remove from oven and sprinkle with nutmeg.

Chocolate Chip Pie

Makes 6-8 servings

30 vanilla wafers (crushed)
¼ cup melted margarine

Mix together and put into a 9-inch pie pan. Bake at 375° for 8 minutes. Let it cool.

1 quart chocolate chip mint ice cream softened

Push the ice cream down into the cooled pie shell. Place in the freezer for about 3 hours. Beat 3 egg whites until foamy; add ½ cup sugar to the egg white mixture. Beat until stiff and shiny. Place the meringue over the ice cream making sure it is sealed. Bake for 2 minutes at 500°. Serve right away.

Rhubarb Pie

1 9-inch pie crust
3 eggs
3 T. milk
2-2½ cups sugar
¼ cup flour
¾ t. nutmeg
3¼ cups rhubarb, cut up
1 T. butter or margarine

Beat eggs slightly and add milk. Separately mix together sugar, flour, and nutmeg. Then put these two mixtures together and mix. Put rhubarb into uncooked pie crust, pour mixture over top, and dot with butter. Bake at 400° for 50 to 60 minutes.

Impossible Coconut Pie

Put the following ingredients into a blender:

4 eggs
2 cups milk
½ cup flour
½ cup sugar
1 t. vanilla
dash salt
¾ stick butter slightly melted
1 cup coconut

Pour into well-greased 10-inch pie pan. Bake at 350° for 40 minutes.

Peanut Butter Pie

⅓ cup peanut butter
1 cup confectioners' sugar
1 3-ounce package cream cheese, softened
1 9-ounce container whipped topping

Combine all of these ingredients together and put in a graham cracker crust. Very delicious and easy.

Strawberry Pie

1 cup sugar
3 T. cornstarch
pinch salt
1 cup water
2 T. strawberry gelatin
2 t. butter
1 quart strawberries, washed and hulled
1 baked, cooled pie shell

Combine first four ingredients and bring to a boil. Mix dry ingredients and water gradually. Cook for 2 minutes, stirring constantly. Remove from heat. Stir in gelatin and butter. Allow to cool. Fold in fresh berries. Put in pie shell and chill.

Florida Key Lime Pie

1 box chocolate wafers, finely crushed
½ cup butter or margarine
1 can sweetened condensed milk
⅓ cup fresh lime juice
1 T. grated lime rind
3 eggs, separated
3 to 4 drops green food coloring
¼ t. salt
1 cup cream, whipped
2 T. sugar
Shaved chocolate (optional)

Mix crushed wafers and melted butter (or margarine) together. Press firmly to sides and bottom of a 10-inch pie pan. Bake at 350° for 10 minutes. Cool for at least 30 minutes. Meanwhile make the filling by combining milk, lime juice, half of the lime rind, and beaten egg yolks. Add the coloring; mix. Beat the egg whites and salt until stiff (not dry); fold into the other mixture. Pour into the cooled shell and bake at 250° for 10 minutes. Cool and then chill in the refrigerator for at least 30 minutes. Top with whipped cream.

I am so glad that you are here—it helps me realize how beautiful my world is.

French Mint Pie

9-inch baked graham cracker crust
¼ pound butter or margarine
1 cup confectioners' sugar
2 eggs
2 2-ounce squares unsweetened
   chocolate
½ t. peppermint flavoring or 2 drops
   peppermint oil

Cream together butter, confectioners' sugar, and eggs until very smooth. Melt chocolate over hot water (do not scorch) and cool; stir into above mixture. Stir in flavoring (be careful if using the peppermint oil—this is very concentrated). Pour filling into baked crust. Chill at least 12 hours. Serve topped with whipped cream.

Fried Peach Pies
Makes about 10 pies

2 cups unsifted, all-purpose flour
dash ground nutmeg or mace
½ t. salt
1 t. sugar
½ cup margarine
4 or 5 T. cold water
1 t. vinegar
1 quart corn oil for frying peach filling
  (recipe follows)
Confectioners' sugar

1. In bowl, combine flour, nutmeg, salt, and sugar. Cut in margarine with pastry blender or two knives until mixture is well mixed and crumbs form.

2. Sprinkle water and vinegar over mixture while tossing to blend. Press dough firmly into ball with hands. Chill about 1 hour.

3. Divide dough into 10 even portions, rolling each portion out to a 5-inch circle. Place about 2 tablespoons peach filling in each circle, moisten edges of pastry with water, fold over half of pastry to cover, seal, pressing edges together with fork.

4. Pour oil into heavy fryer or skillet, filling utensil no more than ⅓ full. Heat over medium heat to 375°.

5. Carefully put several pies at a time into hot oil and fry until golden brown, 5 to 7 minutes on each side.

6. Drain on absorbent paper. If desired, sprinkle with confectioners' sugar.

Peach Filling

1 pound, about 4, firm, ripe peaches
1 t. ascorbic acid powder (Fruit Fresh)
4 T. sugar
4 t. corn starch
¼ t. cinnamon or nutmeg
⅛ t. ginger

1. Peel peaches and coarsely chop.

2. Combine peaches, ascorbic acid powder, sugar, corn starch, cinnamon and ginger.

Great joys are silent.

Peach Cobbler

¼ cup soft margarine
½ cup sugar
1 cup flour
2 t. baking powder
¼ t. salt
½ cup milk
1 can sliced peaches

Cream margarine and sugar. Sift together flour, baking powder, and salt. Stir into shortening alternately with ½ cup milk. Beat until smooth. Pour into 8-inch square pan. Put over the batter sliced peaches. Lay slices close together. Pour about ¼ cup of the peach juice over the peaches and batter. Bake 45 minutes in about 350° oven.

Serve with milk or ice cream.

Holiday Praline Delight

⅓ cup butter
⅓ cup brown sugar
½ cup chopped pecans
1 baked 9-inch pie shell
1 package vanilla pudding and pie filling. Instant is all right.
1 package Dream Whip

Heat the butter and add the brown sugar and nuts. Pour into the pie shell. Bake at 450° for 5 minutes. Cool. Prepare pie filling as directed for pie. Cool 5 minutes. Stir occasionally. Measure out 1 cup of the pie mixture. Cover with wax paper and chill thoroughly. Pour the remaining pie mixture into the pie shell. Prepare the whipped topping (according to the directions). Fold ⅓ cup of the whipped topping into one cup chilled pie filling. Spread this over the praline and pie mixture. Chill. Garnish with the remaining whipped cream.

Peach-blueberry Pie

1 uncooked pie shell, top and bottom crusts
2 T. lemon juice
3 cups sliced peaches, peeled
1 cup blueberries
1 cup sugar
2 T. quick cooking tapioca
½ t. salt
2 T. butter

Sprinkle lemon juice over mixed fruit. Mix sugar, tapioca, salt, and butter and toss lightly with fruit. Let stand 15 minutes. Turn into pastry shell, mounding in the center. Dot top with butter. Put second crust over fruit and brush top with 1 egg yolk, if desired. Bake at 425° for 45-50 minutes.

Shoo Fly Pie

1½ cups flour
1 t. baking powder
½ cup dark molasses
1 t. soda
¾ cup boiling water
½ cup sugar (brown and white mixed)
4 T. shortening
unbaked pie crust

Combine into a crumb mixture the flour, baking powder, sugar, and shortening. Combine molasses, soda, and boiling water. Pour ⅓ liquid into pastry-lined pie pan. Sprinkle ⅓ of crumbs over liquid. Continue alternating, ending with crumbs. Bake at 350° for 30 minutes.

Apple Brown Betty

6 servings

4 cups large bread crumbs (I prefer a wheat bread)
½ cup melted margarine
¾ t. cinnamon
dash of salt
¾ cup brown sugar
4 cups chopped cooking apples

Grease a 1½-quart baking dish. Preheat oven to 375°. Combine bread crumbs with butter, cinnamon, salt, and sugar. Toss lightly. Make alternate layers of crumb mixture and apples in baking dish, ending with bread crumbs. Bake about 1 hour, or until top is a rich golden brown and apples are tender. Serve warm with cream.

Cherry Crisp

¼ cup flour
¾ cup cherry juice
¼ t. red coloring
1 cup sugar
salt
1 can cherries
1½ cups flour
½ t. baking soda
¼ t. salt
¾ cup raw quick oats
1 cup brown sugar
½ cup shortening

Cook ½ cup flour, cherry juice, red coloring, sugar, salt, and cherries. Make crumb mix by sifting 1½ cups flour, baking soda, salt. Add to raw quick oats, brown sugar, and shortening, making crumbs. Put half of crumb mix into a baking dish, add cherries, then remainder of crumb mix. Bake at 350° for 25 to 30 minutes in a 12x8x2-inch or 13x9x2-inch pan.

BREADS

Breads

Breads, Rolls, Buns, Pancakes

The simplest meal is given a delightful lift with homemade bread. Yeast rolls, either plain or sweet, are no trick to make; with a good basic yeast dough recipe many adaptations may be made. Any effort on your part will be well worth it in the words of praise you will receive.

Anadama Bread

7 to 8 cups all-purpose flour (unsifted)
1¼ cups yellow cornmeal
2½ t. salt
2 packages active dry yeast
⅓ cup butter, softened
⅔ cup molasses

In large bowl of electric mixer thoroughly combine 2½ cups flour with the cornmeal, salt, and yeast. Add softened butter and molasses. Gradually add 2½ cups very warm tap water and beat 2 minutes at medium speed of electric mixer, scraping bowl occasionally. Add ½ cup flour. Beat at high speed 2 minutes, scraping bowl occasionally. Stir in enough additional flour to make a stiff dough. Turn out onto a lightly floured board and knead until smooth and elastic (about 8 to 10 minutes). Place in

a greased bowl, turning once to grease top. Cover; let rise in a warm place, free from draft, until doubled in bulk, about 1 hour. Grease two 9x5x3-inch loaf pans. When dough has doubled in bulk, punch it down and divide in half. Shape into loaves and place in loaf pans. Cover; let rise in a warm place, free from draft until doubled in bulk, about 45 minutes. While loaves are rising, preheat oven to 375°. Bake 45 minutes or until done. Remove from pans and cool on wire racks.

Aebleskiver

2 cups buttermilk
2 cups flour
3 eggs
1 t. baking powder
½ t. salt
2 t. sugar
applesauce—if desired

Beat the egg yolks. Add sugar, salt, and milk; then flour, baking soda, and baking powder which have been sifted together. Last fold in stiffly beaten egg whites. Place a small amount of grease in each cup of the aebleskiver pan and fill ⅔ full of batter. If using applesauce, place a small amount on top of the batter, then barely cover the applesauce with a few drops of batter. Cook until bubbly; turn carefully and finish baking on the other side. Serve with butter and maple syrup, jam, or confectioners' sugar (butter may be omitted). Avoid spilling the applesauce in the cups as this will cause the aebleskiver to stick.

Applesauce Muffins

Makes 12 muffins.

1¼ cups flour
3 t. baking powder
½ t. salt
2 T. sugar
1 cup all-bran cereal
1 beaten egg
⅓ cup milk
⅔ cup applesauce
¼ cup melted shortening

Sift together the flour, baking powder, salt, and sugar; blend in all-bran cereal. In another bowl blend: beaten egg, milk, applesauce, and shortening. Mix all ingredients and fill greased muffin tins ⅔ full. Bake 20 minutes at 400°.

Banana Nut Bread

½ cup shortening
2 eggs
2 cups flour
1 t. salt
½ t. vanilla
1 cup sugar
1½ cups mashed bananas
  (3 large ones)
1 t. soda
⅔ cup chopped nuts

Cream shortening and sugar. Add beaten eggs, mix well. Add bananas. Add dry ingredients, vanilla, and nuts. Makes two small loaves. Put in greased pans and bake one hour at 300° to 325°. Use plain or iced.

Blueberry Coffee Cake
Makes 9 large pieces.

1 egg
½ cup sugar
1¼ cups sifted flour
2 t. baking powder
¾ t. salt
⅓ cup milk
3 T. melted butter
1 cup fresh blueberries
2 T. sugar

Night before: Lightly grease 8x8x2-inch pan. Beat egg with wooden spoon, then gradually add ½ cup sugar, beating until well combined. Sift together flour, baking powder, salt. Add to sugar mixture alternately with milk—beat well after each addition. Add the melted butter and beat thoroughly. Then gently fold in blueberries. Pour into pan. Sprinkle top with 2 tablespoons sugar. Refrigerate over night.

Next day: Bake at 350° 30-35 minutes. Brush top with butter and serve warm.

Blueberry Muffins

¾ cup sugar
½ cup shortening (part butter)
2 eggs, separated
2⅓ cups flour
2 t. baking powder
½ t. salt
1 cup milk
1 cup blueberries

Cream sugar and shortening together. Add egg yolks and mix well. Add baking powder and salt to flour and stir to blend. Set aside ½ cup of blended dry ingredients. Add remaining dry ingredients, alternately with milk, to creamed mixture. Beat egg whites until stiff, and fold into batter. Dredge the blueberries in ½ cup of blended dry ingredients, and fold mixture into batter. Fill greased muffin cups ⅔ full. Bake for 20 to 25 minutes at 400°.

Bran Muffins

1 cup all-bran cereal
¾ cup milk
1 egg
¼ cup soft shortening
1 cup sifted flour
2½ t. baking powder
½ t. salt
¼ cup sugar

Combine bran and milk. Let stand until most of the moisture is taken up. Add egg and shortening and beat well.

In second bowl sift together flour, baking powder, salt, and sugar. Add to first mixture, stirring only until combined. Fill greased muffin pans ⅔ full. Bake in moderate oven (375°) about 30 minutes. If sour milk or buttermilk is used, reduce baking powder to 1 teaspoon and add ½ teaspoon baking soda.

Sugar Biscuits

Sift into bowl:

2 cups flour
1 cup sugar
2 t. baking powder

Mix in:

4 T. butter or margarine

Break into a 1 cup measuring cup 1 egg and then fill the rest of the cup with milk. Add this to the above dry ingredients. The more you mix the batter the finer the texture will be. Fill paper muffin cups or well-greased muffin tins half full. Bake at 375° for 20 minutes or until light brown on top.

Cinnamon Crisps

Mix together:

2 sticks melted butter
1 cup sugar
1 egg yolk (save the white)

Sift together and add to the above:

2 (scant) cups flour
4 heaping t. cinnamon

Spread on a buttered cookie sheet or jelly roll pan. Spread it thinly—¼ inch or less in thickness. Brush the top with slightly beaten egg white and cover thickly with chopped pecans. Press them down into the batter. Bake at 400° 15 or 20 minutes, but watch closely. Cut in bars while they are still warm. They will become quite crisp and chewy after cooking.

Yankee Doughnuts

2 cups Bisquick
2 T. sugar
1 t. vanilla
1 egg
¼ cup milk
¼ t. cinnamon
¼ t. nutmeg

Heat the cooking oil in a pan (or in miniature fryer) 3 to 4 inches deep. Mix all the ingredients until smooth. Gently smooth the dough into a ball on a floured cloth-covered board. Knead 8 to 10 times. Roll out the dough ¼ inch thick. Cut with a floured doughnut cutter and drop the rings into the hot fat. Fry about ½ minute on each side or until golden brown. Drain. If desired sprinkle with cinnamon sugar or ice with confectionary frosting.

I still believe in tomorrow.

Corn Bread

1 cup flour
1 cup yellow cornmeal
4 t. baking powder
½ t. salt
½ cup sugar
1 egg
1 cup milk
½ cup soft shortening

Sift dry ingredients into a medium bowl. Add milk, egg, and shortening. Beat with egg beater 1 minute. Don't overbeat. Bake 20 to 25 minutes at 425°.

Norwegian Pancakes

1 cup flour
¼ t. salt
1 T. melted butter
1 t. vanilla or lemon extract
1 T. sugar
3 eggs, separated
2 cups milk

Sift flour, salt, and sugar together. Beat egg yolks; add milk and flavoring. Next, add flour mixture and melted butter. Last, fold in stiffly beaten egg whites. Put small amount of batter in hot greased skillet and tip skillet until batter covers entire surface. Turn when light tan on one side; cook other side. Take out and roll like little log. To serve, unroll, smear with butter, and sprinkle generously with powdered sugar; then reroll and eat. Not for calorie-conscious people.

Coffee Cake

1 package butter golden cake mix
½ cup sugar
4 eggs
1 small carton sour cream
¾ cup liquid oil

Topping

4 T. brown sugar
¾ cup chopped nuts
2 t. cinnamon

Add sour cream, cake mix, sugar, and oil, then add eggs one at a time. Hand beat. Grease and flour a large tube pan or Bundt pan. Spread half the batter in the pan then add half of the topping mixture, the rest of the batter and end with the topping mixture. Bake at 325° for one hour.

Fear not that thy life shall come to an end, but rather fear that it shall never have a beginning.

—*J. H. Newman*

Spoon Bread

3 cups milk
3 eggs
1¼ cups cornmeal
2 T. butter
1¾ t. baking powder
1 t. salt

Bring the milk to a boil and stir in the cornmeal, stirring constantly. Continue stirring until thick. Cool. Add the beaten eggs and other ingredients. Beat 10-15 minutes with an electric beater at medium speed. Bake 30-35 minutes at 375° in a well-greased casserole. One cup of sharp grated cheddar cheese may be added to this mixture.

Mama Smith's Biscuits

Makes 6 biscuits

½ cup buttermilk
1 large T. shortening
1 t. baking powder (heaping teaspoon)
almost 1 cup flour
⅛ t. salt

Mix dry ingredients together and then cut in shortening. Add buttermilk. Knead, roll and cut out. Bake in hot oven.

Mama always put 2 tablespoons sugar in a large can of baking powder. I don't know a specific reason but I do know that sometimes we called them "angel" biscuits they were so light and good. It was the bread for breakfast for over sixty years.

Kentucky Corn Sticks

Makes about 12.

1 cup milk
⅛ t. baking soda
¼ t. salt
1 t. baking powder
1 T. sugar
½ cup flour
1 cup corn meal
1 egg, slightly beaten

Preheat oven to 425°. Grease corn stick pans. Combine the first five ingredients. Stir until the sugar is dissolved. Add the flour and corn meal. Stir until smooth. Add egg and beat well. Spoon the batter into the pans (about ¾ full). Bake 20 minutes.

A mouse perched jauntily on an elephant's back crossed a rickety bridge. The mouse said, "Didn't we make that bridge shake?"

Cinnamon Loaves

1 cup sugar
½ cup shortening
2 eggs
1 t. vanilla
1 cup dairy sour cream
¼ cup milk
2 cups all-purpose flour
1½ t. baking powder
1 t. baking soda
½ t. salt
¼ cup sugar
2 t. cinnamon
1½ t. finely shredded orange peel

Cream together the 1 cup sugar and the shortening until light and fluffy. Add the eggs and vanilla; beat well. Blend in sour cream and milk. Sift together flour, baking powder, soda, and salt; add to creamed mixture. Mix well. Spread ¼ of the batter into each of two greased 7½x3½x2-inch baking pans. Combine the remaining sugar, the cinnamon, and orange peel. Sprinkle all but 1 tablespoon over the batter in pans. Top each with remaining batter. Cut through batter gently with knife to make swirling effect with cinnamon. Top with remaining sugar mixture. Bake in 350° oven 35 to 40 minutes. Makes 2 loaves or for one large loaf, bake in a 9x5x3-inch loaf pan for 45 to 50 minutes.

Hush Puppies
Makes 6 to 8 hush puppies.

1 cup corn meal
2 t. baking powder
1 t. sugar
2 T. flour
1 t. salt
1 egg
1 small onion, finely chopped
⅓ cup milk

Mix together flour, baking powder, salt, and sugar. Add the corn meal and mix. Add milk, onion, and egg. Stir just until moistened. Drop by tablespoon into deep fat. Cook until desired brownness.

Standard Recipe for Buttermilk Biscuits
About 14 biscuits

2½ cups flour
½ t. salt
½ t. soda
1½ t. baking powder
½ cup shortening
1 cup buttermilk

Sift the dry ingredients and then cut in the shortening. Add buttermilk. Knead, roll, and then cut out. Bake in 450° oven.

Nashville House
Fried Biscuits

Makes about 7 dozen biscuits.

1 quart milk
¼ cup sugar
2⅔ packages dry yeast
½ cup lard or shortening
6 t. salt
7 to 9 cups flour

Add yeast to warm water. Add other ingredients and let dough rise. Work into biscuits and drop into hot fat. The fat should be slightly hotter than 350°. If fat is too hot, the biscuits will be soggy in the center. When you work them up, don't let the biscuits rise too high. They can be frozen individually and stored in plastic bags.

Drop Dumplings

1 cup flour
2 t. baking powder
1 t. salt
2 T butter
½ cup fine, dry bread crumbs
1 beaten egg
⅔ cup milk
2 t. grated onion

Sift together the flour, baking powder, and salt; then cut in butter. Add bread crumbs. Blend in 1 beaten egg, milk, and grated onion. Mix only until moistened. Drop batter onto hot liquid. Cover and steam for 20 minutes.

Maryland Beaten Biscuits

2 cups all purpose flour
½ t. salt
1 t. sugar
pinch baking powder

Sift above ingredients together twice. Add 1 tablespoon shortening, worked well into the flour, adding just enough water to make a very stiff dough. You can beat about 1,000 beats or knead or grind with meat grinder until dough pops. Make in small balls; prick with fork. Have oven heated to very hot (about 500°); bake 20 minutes on heavy bottom griddle. Makes 20 or 22 biscuits, depending upon how large you make them. They should be a golden brown. Don't let them touch on the griddle; have a space between each biscuit. This is a very old recipe from a woman in Baltimore.

Generosity consists not in the sum given, but in the manner in which it is bestowed.

Chocolate Yankee Doughnuts

Add ¼ cup cocoa to the baking mix for the original Yankee doughnuts. Increase the sugar to ¼ cup and milk to ⅜ cup. Omit the cinnamon and nutmeg.

Chocolate Glaze—Melt 2 ounces semisweet chocolate and 3 tablespoons butter or margarine over low heat. Remove from heat and stir in 1 cup confectioners' sugar and ¾ teaspoon vanilla. Mix in 2 to 3 tablespoons water. Add water one tablespoon at a time until glaze is proper consistency.

Heirloom Boston Brown Bread

2 cups buttermilk
½ cup molasses
2 cups whole wheat flour
½ cup sifted all-purpose flour
2 t. baking soda
1 t. salt
1 cup seedless raisins (optional)

Grease two 1-pound coffee cans (or something the same size). Combine buttermilk and molasses. Sift together the dry ingredients and stir in the raisins (if using them). Stir in the buttermilk mixture and then spoon the batter into the cans. Bake in a 350° oven for 40 to 50 minutes. Cool on wire racks. Delicious served with softened cream cheese.

Quick Crescent Caramel Pecan Rolls

5 T. butter
¾ cup brown sugar
¼ cup water
½ cup chopped pecans
2 8-ounce cans crescent rolls
3 T. butter
¼ cup sugar
2 T. cinnamon

Preheat oven to 375°. Melt the 5 tablespoons butter in a 13x9x2-inch pan in the oven. Stir in brown sugar, water, and pecans. Separate each can of dough into 4 rectangles and seal perforations. Spread with 3 tablespoons softened butter. Sprinkle combined sugar and cinnamon over dough. Starting at shorter side roll up each rectangle. Cut each roll into 4 slices forming 32 pieces. Place cut side down in prepared pan. Bake at 375° for 20 to 25 minutes until golden brown. Invert pan immediately. Serve warm.

Miniature Cherry Nuts

1 8-ounce package cream cheese
2 sticks margarine
1½ cups sugar
1½ t. vanilla
4 eggs
2¼ cups sifted flour
1½ t. baking powder
1 8-ounce jar well-drained and
   chopped maraschino cherries
½ cup chopped pecans

Topping:

1½ cups confectioners' sugar
1-2 T. milk
pecans
red and green maraschino cherries

Grease two miniature muffin tins. Heat oven to 350°. Thoroughly blend softened cream cheese, margarine, sugar and vanilla. Add eggs, one at a time, mixing well after each time. Gradually add 2 cups flour that had been sifted with the baking powder. Combine the remaining flour with the cherries and pecans; fold into batter. Spoon the batter into the miniature muffin tins about ⅔ full. Bake 20 to 25 minutes or until lightly browned. Cool then frost with confectioners' sugar glaze. Cut red and green maraschino cherries in half.

Garnish the tops with cherries or half pecans.

Basic Yeast Bread Recipe for Rolls, Buns or Coffee Cake

2 cakes yeast
3 T. lard
1 T. butter
1 cup lukewarm water
1¼ t. salt
4 T. sugar
1 pint warm milk
approximately 2 pounds flour

Soften yeast in 1 cup of lukewarm water. Scald milk (1 pint); add sugar, salt, lard, and butter—all mixed together. Then add dissolved yeast to flour and mix well by kneading until smooth and elastic. Place in lightly greased bowl, cover with cloth and let rise in a warm place (75° to 95°) until double in bulk, about 2 hours. Punch down and form into shape desired. Place on greased baking sheets, 1½ inches apart. Let rise again in warm place until double in bulk. Bake 15 to 20 minutes in hot oven at 400°.

Each must find his own road.

Refrigerator Rolls

1 cake yeast
2 T. lukewarm water
½ cup sugar
2 cups scalded milk (cooled to
   lukewarm)
2 beaten eggs
1 t. salt
6 cups flour
¾ cup melted shortening, lukewarm

Dissolve yeast and sugar in 2 tablespoons of lukewarm water. Mix in the milk, eggs, and salt. Add part of flour—do not knead. Add melted shortening and mix well. Add rest of flour; mix until smooth.

Cover and let stand in refrigerator overnight. Take out. Roll in thirds (not too thin). Cut into 12 wedges. Put wedges on greased cookie sheet. Let stand 3 hours in a warm place. Bake 15 minutes at 425°. (When rolling, start at outer edge and roll toward center.)

Easy Caramel Orange Ring

1 T. butter, softened
½ cup orange marmalade
2 T. chopped nuts
1 cup firmly packed brown sugar
½ t. cinnamon
2 10-ounce cans refrigerated
   buttermilk biscuits
½ cup butter, melted.

Preheat oven to 350°. Grease bundt pan with 1 tablespoon butter. Place teaspoonsful of orange marmalade in pan. Sprinkle with nuts. Combine brown sugar and cinnamon; mix well and set aside. Separate biscuits. Dip biscuits in melted butter, then sugar mixture. Stand biscuits on edge in pan. Sprinkle with remaining sugar mixture and drizzle with remaining butter. Bake at 350° for 30-40 minutes or until brown. Cool upright in pan for 5 minutes; invert onto serving plate.

Our mind and body seem to be a delicate related whole, and more and more we are coming to know that we can control, through our thinking, many of the body functions and malfunctions. Biofeedback is making great strides as we learn to concentrate and *will* our blood pressure to lower, relax and let the headache disappear, think consciously of the heart slowing. We are in control over much of the way we feel. Relaxing is one way to gain new strength and energy in a brief few minutes. Progressive relaxation is easy to do and can be done almost anywhere. Yoga has many exercises that help in relieving stress, strain, and fatigue. It will help beautify, strengthen, and give calmness to the body and spirit. And it is so easy. Are you ready?

Get in a comfortable position. Sitting on a chair or lying on a floor, consciously pay attention to your breathing. This is basic. Take a deep breath and let the abdomen expand; then exhale slowly. Some open the mouth slightly when they exhale. Do this several times. Then consciously think of a force of energy coming up as you inhale and let it go down through your body and out through your legs and feet as you exhale. Begin then at the top of your head and consciously (this is most important) think of each part of your body and actually tell it to relax. Feel it. Experience it. Move down to the eyes, ears, mouth (let your lower jaw hang a little loose). Your neck is very important. Let your head hang down slightly if you are sitting and experience it going limp. Then think of your shoulders, your arms and hands; move consciously, silently

talking to each part of your chest, abdomen, hips, thighs, knees, calves, ankles, and feet. Remember to keep up the deep breathing. Just let the problems and pressures of your world go. Relax. Other helps as you totally relax at this point will include:

—breathe in the good air; exhale the bad.
—breathe in the beautiful; exhale the ugly.
—breathe in strength; exhale weakness.
—breathe in confidence; exhale inability.
—breathe in the positive; exhale negative.
—breathe in calmness; exhale tension.

If you aren't asleep by this time, just sit or lie there for a moment and think of beautiful scenery—the most beautiful place you have ever been—and in your mind's eye transport yourself there again. Feel it? Enjoy it! Then slowly return to your workaday world. You will feel renewed and refreshed. And it is done without tranquilizers, alcohol, or sleeping pills. You are in control, not under the crutch influence. Do it daily. You'll love it!

Glazed Apple Cookies
Makes about 3 dozen cookies.

½ cup butter
1⅓ cups brown sugar
1 egg
2 cups sifted flour
1 t. baking soda
½ t. salt
1 t. cinnamon
½ t. cloves
¼ t. nutmeg
1 cup coarsely ground pecans
1 cup finely chopped, peeled apples
1 cup raisins
¼ cup milk

Glaze:

1½ cups sifted confectioners' sugar
1 T. butter
½ t. vanilla
2½ T. milk

Beat together butter and brown sugar until light and fluffy. Beat in egg to blend thoroughly. Sift together flour, salt, baking soda, and spices. Stir half of dry ingredients into creamed mixture. Stir in nuts, apples, and raisins. Then stir in remaining dry ingredients and milk. Mix well. Drop from tablespoon 1½ inches apart onto lightly greased baking sheet. Bake 10 to 12 minutes in 400° oven.

Remove to cooling racks and while still warm spread with glaze.

Peanut Butter Drops

1 cup sugar
1 cup light corn syrup
½ cup peanut butter
1 cup Special K cereal
1 cup thin pretzels, broken

Mix sugar and syrup in large sauce pan. Bring to boil over medium heat; cook for about 30 seconds. Remove from heat and add peanut butter; stir until smooth. Add cereal and pretzels; mix. Drop by spoonful on wax paper.

Peanut Butter Cookies

½ cup shortening
½ cup granulated sugar
½ cup peanut butter
½ cup brown sugar
1 egg
1¼ cups flour
¾ t. baking powder
¼ t. soda

Cream together shortening, granulated sugar, peanut butter, and brown sugar. Add 1 well-beaten egg. Beat well. Sift dry ingredients, and add to the butter and egg mixture. Mix thoroughly; chill for ½ hour. Roll into small ball shapes about size of a walnut. Place on greased cookie sheet an inch apart. Flatten each ball with a fork, crisscrossing the cookie. Bake in moderate oven 10 minutes.

Soft Sugar Cookies

2 eggs
1½ cups sugar
1 cup shortening
1 cup milk (sweet)
1 t. vanilla
4 cups flour
2 t. baking powder
2 t. cream of tartar
2 scant t. soda

Beat eggs 1 minute. Add sugar and shortening and beat 1 minute. Add vanilla and milk. Sift dry ingredients and combine with first mixture. Drop by spoon onto cookie sheet and bake 6 to 8 minutes at 375°. When cool frost with powdered sugar icing.

Frosting

6 T. room temperature butter
⅛ t. salt
1 pound confectioners sugar
2 t. vanilla
4 to 5 T. milk

Put all ingredients in bowl and beat at high speed 1 minute. Divide icing into several parts and color each with food coloring. Makes variety out of one batch of cookies.

Cheesecake Cookies
Makes about 16 cookies.

⅓ cup packed brown sugar
1 cup flour
½ cup walnuts, chopped
⅓ cup melted butter
1 8-ounce package cream cheese
¼ cup granulated sugar
1 egg
1 T. lemon juice
2 T. milk
1 t. vanilla

Mix brown sugar, flour, and nuts together in a large bowl. Stir in the melted butter and mix with your hands until light and crumbly. Remove 1 cup of the mixture to be used later as a topping. Place remainder in an 8-inch square pan and press firmly. Bake at 350° for about 12-15 minutes.

Beat cream cheese with the granulated sugar until smooth. Beat in the egg, lemon juice, milk, and vanilla. Pour this into the baked crust. Top with the reserved crumbs. Return to 350° oven and bake for about 25 minutes. Cool thoroughly; then cut into 2-inch squares.

Peanut Butter Kiss Cookies
Makes about 3 dozen.

½ cup butter
½ cup peanut butter
½ cup sugar
½ cup firmly packed brown sugar

Cream the above ingredients together well. Add:

1 unbeaten egg
1 t. vanilla
1¾ cups sifted flour

Shape into round balls and roll in granulated sugar. Place on an ungreased cookie sheet and bake at 375° for 8 minutes. Take out of the oven and place chocolate kisses on the cookies. Press in and bake 2-5 minutes longer.

Butter Cookies

5 cups flour
4 eggs
1 pound butter
2 cups sugar
1½ t. baking powder
⅛ t. salt
2 t. vanilla

Cream eggs, butter, and sugar. Add sifted dry ingredients and vanilla. Chill until dough is hard. Roll thin, cut with favorite cookie cutter and bake 8 to 10 minutes in 350° oven. There is no water or milk in these butter cookies.

Date-Coconut Bars
Makes 35 bars.

½ cup packed brown sugar
¼ cup butter or margarine
1 cup chopped dates
1 egg, slightly beaten
2½ cups crisp rice cereal
1 cup flaked coconut

In 3-quart saucepan combine sugar, butter, dates, and egg. Stir over low heat until mixture is slightly thickened and foamy, about 5 minutes; cool. Stir in cereal and coconut. Pack evenly in 8-inch square foil or baking pan; cool. Cut in 1½x1-inch bars.

Brown Edge Cookies

½ cup butter (¼ pound)
⅓ cup sugar
1 egg, well beaten
¾ cup flour
1 t. vanilla

Mix all ingredients and drop on buttered cookie sheet one inch apart. Bake slowly at 325°. If desired, place nuts or raisins in center of each cookie.

Pecan Cookies
Makes 3½ dozen.

Preheat oven to 300°. In medium bowl, with electric mixer at high speed, beat 2 egg whites until stiff but not dry. Gradually beat in 2 cups sifted confectioners' sugar, 1 teaspoon vinegar and 1 teaspoon vanilla extract. Fold in 2 cups pecan halves. Drop teaspoonfuls of dough, 2 inches apart, on greased cookie sheets. Bake 12 to 15 minutes. (Cookies remain light.) Remove from sheets at once; cool.

Whatever my secrets are, remember when I entrust them to you, they are part of me.

Ice Box Cookies

2 cups brown sugar
1 cup melted butter or margarine
  (½ pound)
2 eggs
3½ cups sifted flour
1 cup black walnuts

Cream sugar, butter, and eggs. Add nuts, and stir in flour. Make several rolls. Put in ice box 10 hours. Slice and bake in moderate oven.

Thumbprint Cookies

½ cup soft shortening
¼ cup brown sugar
1 cup flour
¼ t. salt
1 egg, separated
½ t. vanilla
¾ cup finely chopped nuts
jelly or confectioners' sugar

Blend shortening, brown sugar, egg yolk, and vanilla. Sift the flour and salt, and stir into first mixture. Roll into 1-inch balls. Dip in slightly beaten egg whites. Roll in finely chopped nuts. Place about 1 inch apart on ungreased baking sheet. Bake 5 minutes at 375°. Remove from oven and quickly press thumb gently on top of each cookie. Return to oven and bake 8 minutes longer. Cool. Place sparkling jelly or tinted confectioners' sugar icing in thumbprints.

Oatmeal Cookies
Makes about 3 dozen.

2 cups quick-cooking rolled oats
¾ cup sugar
½ cup butter or margarine, melted and
  cooled
¼ cup flour
2 egg whites, stiffly beaten

In mixing bowl stir together oats, sugar, butter, and flour. Fold in egg whites until well blended; drop by heaping teaspoonfuls on greased cookie sheets. Bake in preheated 350° oven until golden, about 12 minutes. Remove to rack to cool. Store in airtight container.

French Buttercream Cookies

Makes 4 dozen.

1½ cups powdered sugar
1 t. soda
1 t. cream of tartar
¼ t. salt
1 cup softened butter or margarine
1 egg
1 t. vanilla
2¼ cups flour

In a large bowl combine the first 7 ingredients on low speed of mixer, about 1 minute. Blend well. Gradually add flour. Blend at low speed until well mixed. If desired, tint dough with a few drops of food coloring.

Chill dough 15-30 minutes before shaping. Shape into ¾-inch balls; place on greased cookie sheet about 2 inches apart. Flatten balls with fork, sprinkle with colored sugars. Bake at 350° for 5-8 minutes until set but not brown. Let cookies stand on cookie sheet 1 minute; cool on racks.

Baked Fudge Cookies

¼ cup milk
2 ounces chocolate
⅓ cup shortening
1 cup sugar
½ cup flour
1 t. vanilla
2 eggs
½ t. salt
1 cup nutmeats

Heat milk and melt chocolate and shortening in it. Mix in a bowl the remaining ingredients. Combine contents of pan and bowl. Spread on greased 12x16-inch pan. Bake 10 minutes in 325° oven. Remove from oven and spread on chocolate icing. Cut in squares when cold.

Icing: Mix together 1½ tablespoons melted butter, 1¼ cups confectioners' sugar, 1 teaspoon vanilla, and 2 squares chocolate (melted). If necessary, add evaporated milk for easier spreading.

"My business is not to remake myself, but to make the absolute best of what God made."
—Robert Browning

Barb's Brownies

6 eggs
3 cups sugar
2 cups flour
2 sticks (1 cup)
melted margarine
¾ cup cocoa
2 t. vanilla

Mix the eggs, sugar and flour together. Melt the margarine and add the cocoa. Stir until well blended. Combine the eggs, sugar and flour with the cocoa-margarine mixture. Add the vanilla.

Bake at 425° for 15 minutes in a greased jelly roll pan, 10x15-inch or 9x13-inch.

*These are very moist and do need to be watched closely so they do not overbake.

Lemon-Walnut Refrigerator Cookies

Makes about 4 dozen.

1 10- or 11-ounce box piecrust mix
⅔ cup sugar
grated peel of 1 lemon
1 egg
1 T. lemon juice
½ cup finely chopped walnuts or other nuts

Combine mix, sugar, and lemon peel. Beat egg and lemon juice and stir into mix until moist and crumbly. Add walnuts and, with fingers, work into dough. Shape in 12-inch log, wrap in waxed paper and chill at least 1 hour. Cut in ¼-inch slices and bake in preheated 350° oven 12 to 15 minutes or until golden.

Praline Confection

20-24 graham crackers
1 cup butter or margarine
1 cup light brown sugar, packed
1 cup chopped pecans

Line a 15x10x1-inch baking sheet with whole crackers. Bring sugar and butter to a rolling boil and boil 2 minutes. Remove from heat; when bubbling stops, add the nuts. Spoon over crackers. Bake at 350° for 10 minutes. Cool slightly; cut into squares.

A conscience, like a buzzing bee, can make a fellow uneasy without ever stinging him.
—Am. Farm Almanac

Marbled Brownies

2 3-ounce packages cream cheese
5 T. margarine
⅓ cup sugar
2 eggs
2 T. flour
¾ t. vanilla
1 family-size package brownie mix

Frosting:

3 T. margarine
2 T. cocoa
1½ cups powdered sugar
2 T. milk
1 t. vanilla

Beat together the first 2 ingredients. Add the next four ingredients and beat until smooth. Set aside. Prepare the cake-like brownie batter as directed on the package. Pour ½ the brownie batter into a greased 13x9-inch pan. Pour all the cream cheese mixture over the brownie layer. Spoon rest of brownie batter in spots over top. Swirl with a knife. Bake at 350° for 35-40 minutes.

Melt butter for frosting in saucepan. Stir in cocoa until dissolved. Add powdered sugar, milk, and vanilla. Stir until smooth. Add more milk if necessary.

Snickerdoodles
Makes 5 dozen.

1 cup shortening (part butter)
1½ cups sugar
2 eggs
2¾ cups flour
2 t. cream of tartar
1 t. soda
¼ t. salt
2 T. sugar
2 t. cinnamon

Sift the flour, tartar, soda, and salt. Mix the shortening, sugar, and eggs. Stir the above two mixtures together. Roll about 1 teaspoon of dough into a ball and then roll into sugar-cinnamon mixture. Place each ball on ungreased cookie sheet about 1 inch apart. Bake in a 400° oven for 8-10 minutes.

Fudge Brownies

½ cup flour
½ t. salt
⅓ cup shortening
1 cup sugar
1 cup walnuts
½ t. baking powder
3 squares unsweetened chocolate
2 eggs
1 t. vanilla

Melt chocolate and shortening in top of double boiler over boiling water. Remove from water. Beat eggs well, add sugar and vanilla. Mix thoroughly. Stir into melted chocolate and shortening. Add sifted dry ingredients and blend well. Add walnuts; stir just enough to mix. Spread mixture in greased pan, 8x8x2-inches. Bake at 350° for 30 to 35 minutes. Place pan on rack to cool. Cut when thoroughly cool.

Peanut Butter and Cereal Balls

Makes about 3 dozen.

1 cup peanut butter
⅓ cup honey
1 cup crunchy wheat and barley cereal
   nuggets
finely chopped peanuts (optional)

Beat peanut butter and honey until well blended. Stir in cereal. Shape in ½-inch balls and roll in peanuts. Wrap individually in small squares of plastic and keep refrigerated.

Peanut Butter Brownies

2 eggs
1 cup granulated sugar
½ cup brown sugar
¼ cup peanut butter
2 T. margarine
2 t. vanilla
1⅓ cups unsifted flour
1 T. baking powder
½ t. salt
2 T. chopped peanuts

Combine eggs, sugars, peanut butter, margarine and vanilla. Beat at medium speed until thoroughly blended. Add flour, baking powder, and salt and continue mixing until mixture is smooth. Spread batter in a greased 9-inch square pan and sprinkle with chopped peanuts. Bake in moderate oven at 350° for 30 minutes. Cut in squares while warm.

A disagreeable person is one who disagrees with me.

Pecan Cups

Makes 2 dozen.

1 3-ounce package cream cheese,
   softened
½ cup margarine
1 cup flour
1 egg
¾ cup brown sugar
1 T. margarine
½ t. vanilla
dash salt
⅔ cup chopped pecans

Mix the cream cheese, margarine and flour together. Chill for one hour. Then shape into 24 1-inch balls, press balls into miniature muffin tins. Mix the egg, brown sugar, margarine, vanilla, salt, and half the pecans. Pour the mixture into the individual shells. Top each one with a sprinkle of pecans. Bake at 325° for 25 or thirty minutes.

Date and Nut Squares

½ cup shortening
1½ cups brown sugar
½ t. salt
1¼ t. vanilla
1 egg, unbeaten yolk
½ cup coconut
¾ cup sifted all-purpose flour
1 t. baking powder
¾ cup chopped walnuts
½ cup chopped dates

Mix shortening, 1 cup brown sugar, salt, vanilla, and unbeaten egg yolk. Sift flour with baking powder; blend the mixture. Add coconut ½ cup chopped walnuts, and dates. Spread batter in pan evenly. Beat egg white in peaks, beat in remaining sugar and vanilla. Spread on batter with remaining ground walnuts and bake 35 minutes in 325° oven. Cut in squares while hot.

Apricot Squares

Makes 16 cookies.

2/3 cup dried apricots
½ cup butter or margarine, softened
¼ cup granulated sugar
1⅓ cups sifted regular all-purpose flour
½ t. double-acting baking powder
¼ t. salt
1 cup packed light brown sugar
2 eggs
½ cup chopped California walnuts
½ t. vanilla extract
confectioners' sugar

Early in Day:

Cook apricots as label directs; drain and chop finely. Preheat oven to 350°.

In large bowl, cream butter and granulated sugar; stir in 1 cup flour until crumbly; pack mixture into greased 8x8-inch cake pan. Bake 25 minutes or until lightly browned.

Meanwhile, onto waxed paper, sift together ⅓ cup flour, baking powder, and salt. In large bowl, with electric mixer at medium speed, beat brown sugar and eggs until blended; beat in flour mixture, walnuts, vanilla, and apricots. Spread over baked layer and bake 25 to 30 minutes more until golden. Cool on rack; sprinkle lightly with confectioners' sugar. Store, tightly covered.

Seven Layer Cookies

Makes 24 bars.

½ cup butter or margarine
1½ cups graham cracker crumbs
1 can sweetened condensed milk (not evaporated milk)
1 6-ounce package semi-sweet chocolate chips
1 3½ ounce can flaked coconut
1 cup chopped nuts
1 6-ounce package butterscotch chips

In 13x9-inch baking pan, melt butter. Remove from heat. Sprinkle crumbs over butter. Pour sweetened condensed milk evenly over crumbs. Top with chocolate chips, butterscotch chips, coconut, and nuts; press down gently. Bake at 350° for 25 minutes or until golden brown. Cool. Cut into 3x1½-inch bars.

Where love rules there is no will to power.

Williamsburg Inn Pecan Bars

1 cup butter
1 cup light brown sugar, packed
1 cup honey
¼ cup whipping cream
3 cups pecans, chopped (I found 2
    cups to be plenty.)
Sugar Dough partially baked*

Preheat oven to 350°. Put butter, sugar, and honey in deep, heavy-bottomed saucepan; stir and boil 5 minutes. Remove from heat. Cool slightly and add cream and chopped pecans; mix well. Spread topping evenly over surface of the partially baked Sugar Dough with a buttered wooden spoon or flexible spatula. Bake for 30 to 35 minutes at 350°. (I found mine were done after 20 minutes—just check them carefully). Cool and cut into 1x2-inch bars.

*Sugar Dough

¾ cup butter
¾ cup sugar
2 eggs
rind of 1 lemon, grated
3 cups sifted all-purpose flour
½ t. baking powder

Preheat oven to 375° 10 minutes before dough is ready to go into oven. Grease and flour two 9x9x2-inch baking pans. Cream butter and sugar; add eggs and lemon rind and beat well. Sift flour and baking powder together, add to creamed mixture, and beat well. Chill dough until firm enough to handle. Press dough onto bottom and sides of prepared pans. Dough will be approximately ⅛ inch thick. Prick all over with a fork. Bake 12 to 15 minutes at 375° or until dough looks half done. Remove from oven and spread with pecan topping above.

Spicy Apple Twists

Makes 16.

1½ cups sifted all-purpose flour
1 t. salt
½ cup shortening
4-5 T. cold water
or   1 stick pie crust mix

⅓ cup melted margarine
½ cup sugar
1 t. cinnamon
½ cup water
2 baking apples, pared and cored,
   sliced into 8 wedges

Prepare apples. Sift flour with salt into mixing bowl; cut in shortening; sprinkle cold water over mixture, stirring with fork until dough is just moist enough to hold together. Form into ball. Flatten to about ½-inch thickness; smooth edges. Roll out on floured surface to 16x10-inch rectangle. Cut into 16, 10x1-inch strips. Wrap one strip around each apple slice. Arrange in 13x9x2-inch pan, sides not touching. Brush with butter, sprinkle with mixture of sugar and cinnamon. Pour ½ cup water over pastries. Bake in hot oven at 450° for 25-30 minutes, or till golden brown. Serve warm or cold, plain or with cream.

Apple Bars

2½ cups flour
1 cup shortening
¾ t. salt

Mix like a pie crust.
Separate one egg. Add enough milk to yolk to make ⅔ cup. Mix with the above pie crust mixture. Roll out half the pastry; place on a jelly roll pan. Cover with 7 or 8 sliced, peeled apples (Winesap are good). Mix 1⅓ cups sugar, 1 teaspoon cinnamon, 2 tablespoons flour, and 3 tablespoons tapioca. Sprinkle the mixture over the apples and dot with butter. Sprinkle juice of one lemon over the apple mixture. Roll out the other half of the pastry and cover the apples. Beat the egg white and brush over the crust. Bake at 450° for 10 minutes. Turn oven down to 375° and continue baking for 25 minutes. Glaze with a powdered sugar frosting.

Date Pinwheel Cookies

Filling:

1 cup nuts
½ cup sugar
1 pound dates
½ cup water

Use coarse grinder for nuts and dates. Cook all of the above ingredients slowly. Stir, put lid on and let steam for a while. Cool before using.

1 cup shortening
1 cup white sugar
1 cup brown sugar
3 eggs
4 cups flour
1 t. baking powder
1 t. soda
1 t. cinnamon
¼ t. salt
1 t. vanilla

Cream shortening and sugars. Add eggs and mix well. Beat until creamy. Sift dry ingredients, add to mixture. Add vanilla. Roll ¼ inch thick and spread with filling. Roll like jelly roll and put in refrigerator overnight. Slice. Bake 10 minutes at 350°.

Date Bars

½ pound chopped dates
¾ cup water
½ cup sugar
1⅓ cups raw oatmeal
1⅓ cups flour
1 t. soda
1 cup light brown sugar
¾ cup shortening or butter

Cook over low heat the chopped dates, water, and ½ cup sugar. Stir constantly.

Mix together raw oatmeal, flour, and soda. In another bowl combine light brown sugar and shortening or butter. Then combine oatmeal and brown sugar mixtures. Spread layer of dry mixture in 13x9x2-inch baking pan. Add date mixture and top with remaining dry mixture. Bake at 350° for 25 to 30 minutes.

Austrian Chocolate Balls
4 dozen cookies

2 ounces (2 squares) unsweetened chocolate
⅓ cup butter or margarine

Melt together in medium saucepan over low heat. Remove from heat.

1 cup sugar
1 egg plus 1 yolk
½ t. vanilla or almond extract

Stir into chocolate mixture; blend well.

1⅓ cups all purpose flour
½ cup finely chopped nuts

Lightly spoon flour into measuring cup; level off. Gradually stir in flour and nuts until well combined. Shape dough into ¾-inch balls; place on ungreased cookie sheet about 1-inch apart. Bake at 350° for 8 to 12 minutes until firm to the touch (do not overbake). Immediately remove from cookie sheet; cool.

1 ounce (1 square) unsweetened chocolate
1 T. butter or margarine
¼ t. vanilla or almond extract
1 cup powdered sugar
2 or 3 T. milk

In same saucepan, melt chocolate and butter. Remove from heat. Add remaining ingredients; blend well. Dip tops of cookies into glaze to cover. Allow to dry completely before storing cookies tightly covered with waxed paper between layers of cookies.

Russian Tea Cakes
4 dozen cookies

1 cup softened butter or margarine
½ cup powdered sugar
1 t. vanilla
¼ t. salt

In large bowl, combine ingredients on low speed of mixer about 1 minute; blend well.

2¼ cups all-purpose flour

Lightly spoon flour into measuring cup; level off. Gradually add flour at low speed until just combined.

¾ cup finely chopped nuts

Stir in nuts. Roll dough into 1-inch balls; place about 1 inch apart on ungreased cookie sheet. Bake at 350° for 8 to 10 minutes until firm to the touch but not brown (do not overbake). While warm, roll in powdered sugar. Cool; reroll in powdered sugar before serving.